D1419615

HISTORIC SCOTLAND

CASTLES OF SCOTLAND
A VOYAGE THROUGH THE CENTURIES

HISTORIC SCOTLAND

CASTLES OF SCOTLAND
A VOYAGE THROUGH THE CENTURIES

Chris Tabraham

B T Batsford

First published 2005

© Chris Tabraham 2005

The right of Chris Tabraham to be identified as Author of this work has been asserted by him in accordance with the Copyright, Designs and Patents Act 1988.

Volume © B T Batsford Ltd

ISBN 0 7134 8976 6

A CIP catalogue record for this book is available from the British Library.

Printed in Singapore
for the publishers
B T Batsford
Chysalis Books Group
The Chrysalis Building
Bramley Road
London W10 6SP
www.chrysalisbooks.co.uk

A member of Chrysalis Books plc

Distributed in the United States and Canada by Sterling Publishing Co., 387 Park Avenue South, New York, NY 10016, USA

TO LIZ
God bless you

CONTENTS

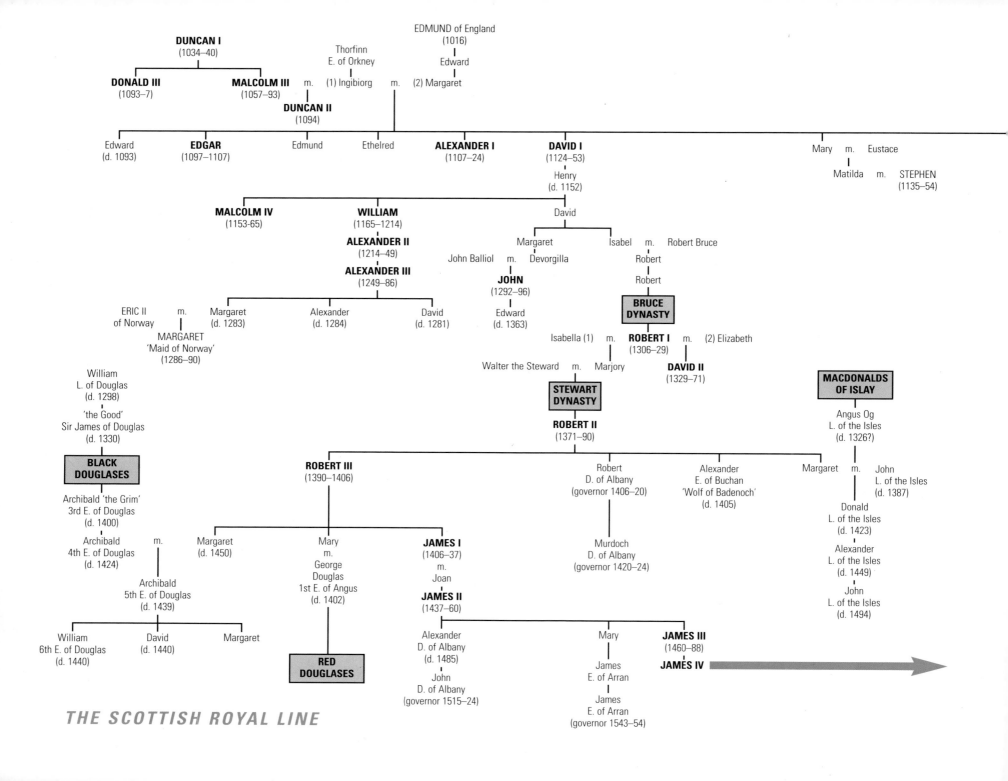

DUNCAN I
(1034–40)

DONALD III
(1093–7)

MALCOLM III
(1057–93)

Thorfinn
E. of Orkney

EDMUND of England
(1016)

Edward

m. (1) Ingibiorg   m. (2) Margaret

DUNCAN II
(1094)

Edward
(d. 1093)

EDGAR
(1097–1107)

Edmund

Ethelred

ALEXANDER I
(1107–24)

DAVID I
(1124–53)

Mary   m.   Eustace

Matilda   m.   **STEPHEN**
(1135–54)

Henry
(d. 1152)

MALCOLM IV
(1153-65)

WILLIAM
(1165–1214)

ALEXANDER II
(1214–49)

ALEXANDER III
(1249–86)

David

Margaret   Isabel   m.   Robert Bruce

John Balliol   m.   Devorgilla

Robert

Robert

JOHN
(1292–96)

**BRUCE
DYNASTY**

ERIC II
of Norway

m.

Margaret
(d. 1283)

Alexander
(d. 1284)

David
(d. 1281)

Edward
(d. 1363)

MARGARET
'Maid of Norway'
(1286–90)

Isabella (1)   m.   **ROBERT I**
(1306–29)

m.   (2) Elizabeth

DAVID II
(1329–71)

**MACDONALDS
OF ISLAY**

William
L. of Douglas
(d. 1298)

'the Good'
Sir James of Douglas
(d. 1330)

Walter the Steward   m.   Marjory

**STEWART
DYNASTY**

ROBERT II
(1371–90)

Angus Og
L. of the Isles
(d. 1326?)

**BLACK
DOUGLASES**

Archibald 'the Grim'
3rd E. of Douglas
(d. 1400)

ROBERT III
(1390–1406)

Robert
D. of Albany
(governor 1406–20)

Alexander
E. of Buchan
'Wolf of Badenoch'
(d. 1405)

Margaret   m.   John
L. of the Isles
(d. 1387)

Archibald
4th E. of Douglas
(d. 1424)

m.

Margaret
(d. 1450)

Mary
m.
George
Douglas
1st E. of Angus
(d. 1402)

JAMES I
(1406–37)
m.
Joan

Murdoch
D. of Albany
(governor 1420–24)

Donald
L. of the Isles
(d. 1423)

Archibald
5th E. of Douglas
(d. 1439)

JAMES II
(1437–60)

Alexander
L. of the Isles
(d. 1449)

William
6th E. of Douglas
(d. 1440)

David
(d. 1440)

Margaret

**RED
DOUGLASES**

Alexander
D. of Albany
(d. 1485)

John
D. of Albany
(governor 1515–24)

Mary

James
E. of Arran

James
E. of Arran
(governor 1543–54)

JAMES III
(1460–88)

JAMES IV

John
L. of the Isles
(d. 1494)

THE SCOTTISH ROYAL LINE

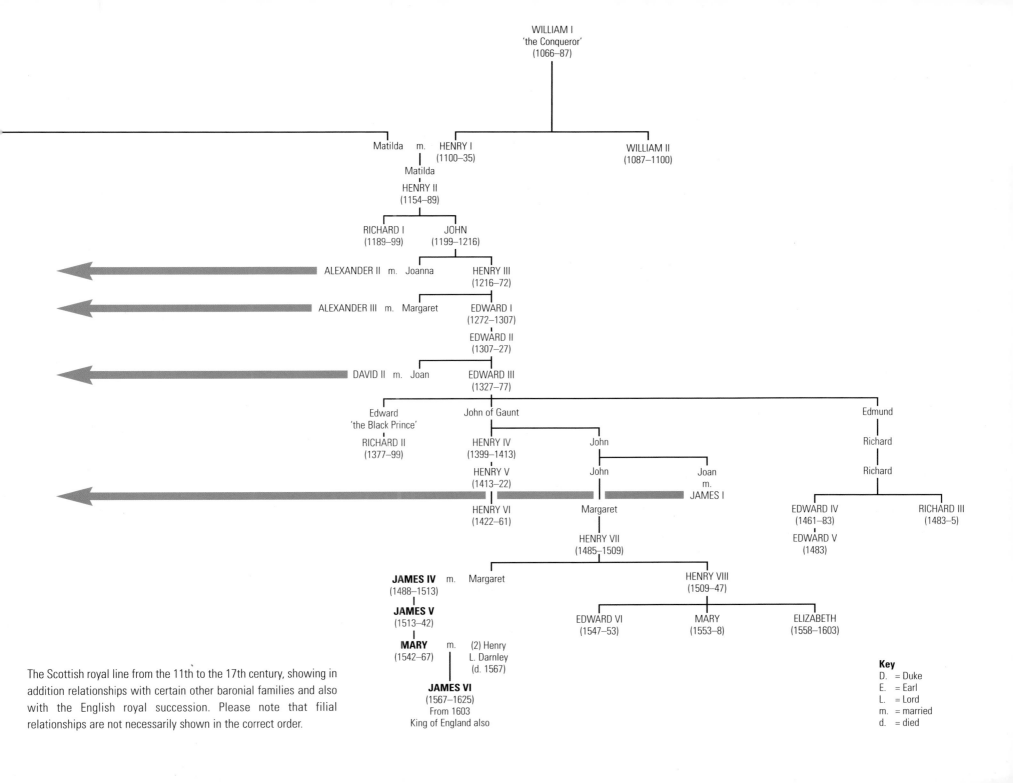

WILLIAM I
'the Conqueror'
(1066–87)

Matilda   m.   HENRY I
(1100–35)

WILLIAM II
(1087–1100)

Matilda
HENRY II
(1154–89)

RICHARD I
(1189–99)

JOHN
(1199–1216)

ALEXANDER II   m.   Joanna

HENRY III
(1216–72)

ALEXANDER III   m.   Margaret

EDWARD I
(1272–1307)

EDWARD II
(1307–27)

DAVID II   m.   Joan

EDWARD III
(1327–77)

Edward
'the Black Prince'

John of Gaunt

Edmund

RICHARD II
(1377–99)

HENRY IV
(1399–1413)

John

Richard

HENRY V
(1413–22)

John

Joan
m.
JAMES I

Richard

HENRY VI
(1422–61)

Margaret

EDWARD IV
(1461–83)

RICHARD III
(1483–5)

HENRY VII
(1485–1509)

HENRY VIII
(1509–47)

EDWARD V
(1483)

JAMES IV   m.   Margaret
(1488–1513)

JAMES V
(1513–42)

EDWARD VI
(1547–53)

MARY
(1553–8)

ELIZABETH
(1558–1603)

MARY   m.   (2) Henry
(1542–67)   L. Darnley
                        (d. 1567)

The Scottish royal line from the 11th to the 17th century, showing in
addition relationships with certain other baronial families and also
with the English royal succession. Please note that filial
relationships are not necessarily shown in the correct order.

JAMES VI
(1567–1625)
From 1603
King of England also

Key
D.   = Duke
E.   = Earl
L.   = Lord
m. = married
d.   = died

Between 1813 and 1823 the artist William Daniell R.A. undertook a voyage around the coast of Great Britain. He published several volumes containing an account of that epic journey, adorned with 'a series of views illustrative of the character and prominent features of the coast'. As far as the Scottish coast was concerned, those views were dominated by castles.

In this book, I follow in Daniell's wake to chart the story of the Scottish castle. Like Daniell, I begin at Caerlaverock on the Solway Firth, thread my way up the Firth of Clyde and through the Inner Hebrides, call in at Kirkwall, capital of the Orkneys, and sail down Scotland's long east coast to Berwick-upon-Tweed. Berwick is in England now, but in the age of castles it was Scottish, and proud of it.

Each of the 30 castles we visit is unique. Yet each also contributes to the full story of the castle in Scotland. We journey through four centuries of castle building.

But our story embraces more than castles. It reaches back into prehistory to the age of the brochs (uniquely Scottish), and comes right up to date with the coastal defences of the modern era. In between, we visit seats of power occupied in the Dark Ages when the nation was being forged, and country seats constructed around the time Scotland was being incorporated into the United Kingdom.

It is a fascinating story encompassing 3000 years. I hope you enjoy this journey through Scotland's past.

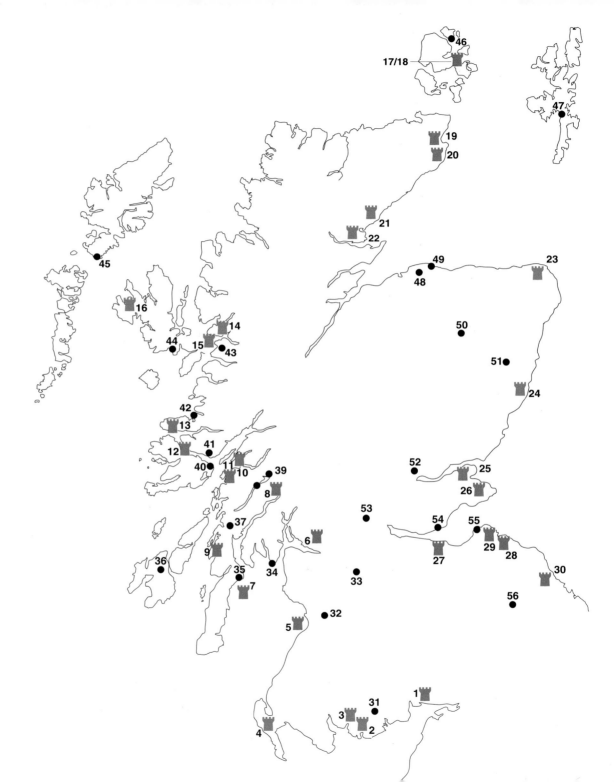

THE CASTLES

1 Caerlaverock Castle
2 MacLellan's Castle
3 Cardoness Castle
4 Dunskey Castle
5 Greenan Castle
6 Dumbarton Castle
7 Lochranza Castle
8 Inverarary Castle
9 Castle Sween
10 Dunollie Castle
11 Dunstaffnage Castle
12 Aros Castle
13 Mingary Castle
14 Eilean Donan Castle
15 Caisteal Maol
16 Dunvegan Castle
17 Bishop's Palace, Kirkwall
18 Earl's Palace, Kirkwall
19 Castle Girnigoe
20 Castle of Old Wick
21 Dunrobin Castle
22 Dornoch Castle
23 Kinnaird Head Castle
24 Dunnottar Castle
25 Broughty Castle
26 St Andrews Castle
27 Edinburgh Castle
28 Tantallon Castle
29 Bass Rock Castle
30 Berwick Castle

OTHER PLACES MENTIONED

31 Threave Castle
32 Dundonald Castle
33 Bothwell Castle
34 Rothesay Castle
35 Skipness Castle
36 Finlaggan
37 Dunadd Fort
38 Innis Chonell Castle
39 Kilchurn Castle
40 Duart Castle
41 Ardtornish Castle
42 Castle Tioram
43 Dun Telve Broch
44 Dun Ringill
45 St Clement's, Rodel
46 Cubbie Roo's Castle
47 Scalloway Castle
48 Duffus Castle
49 Spynie Palace
50 Kildrummy Castle
51 Crathes Castle
52 Huntingtower
53 Stirling Castle
54 Aberdour Castle
55 Dirleton Castle
56 Roxburgh Castle

CAERLAVEROCK CASTLE

Dumfries and Galloway
Border stronghold

Caerlaverock Castle stands on the very edge of Scotland, at the place where the swift-flowing waters of the River Nith enter the treacherous salt marshes of the Solway Firth. To the north lies the rolling Dumfriesshire countryside. Southwards, across the estuary, loom the distant peaks of the English Lake District. Daniell's view (*above*) sets the scene, and Herman Moll's map of 1732 (*see page 12*) gives the location. For over four hundred years, from around 1220 up to the castle's last siege in 1640, the powerful Maxwell

lords held sway from the mighty castle. But long before they arrived in the area, the knuckle of land at the mouth of Nithsdale had served as a border-control point. An Iron-age fortification once crowned the summit of Ward Law, the hill overlooking the castle from the north. So too did the defence that replaced it, a Roman fort (*see right*) measuring almost 3 hectares (7.4 acres) and surrounded by ditches fully 3.5m (12ft) deep. Tacitus, biographer and son-in-law of Gnaeus Julius Agricola, Roman governor of Britain, wrote of a sea-borne

invasion across the Solway in AD 82, and the sands off Caerlaverock may well have been where the legionaries first set foot.

The name Caerlaverock – 'fort of the skylark' – derives from the British word *caer* ('fort', from the Latin *castra*) and the Old English *laewerce* ('lark'), and the British lords of Nithsdale, who filled the vacuum left by the departing legions, may have operated from a base near where the present castle stands. In the mid-12th century, when Dumfriesshire and Cumberland were united under one ruler, David I of Scotland, Radulph son of Dunegal, lord of Strath Nith, granted lands at 'Karlaueroc' to the monks of the newly founded Holm Cultram Abbey, on the southern (Cumbrian) shore of the Solway. But King David's death in 1153 effectively ended Scotland's control over Cumbria, and within fifty years the final curtain had been drawn on the Celtic overlordship of Nithsdale too. Into Radulph's shoes stepped an incomer from eastern Scotland, Sir John de Maccuswell (Maxwell).

Caerlaverock has not one but two medieval castles. The older of the two was built by the Maxwells soon after they arrived in the region in the 1220s. Excavation has recently shown it to have been quadrangular in plan; projecting towers were subsequently added to three of the four corners. However, the Caerlaverock Castle that so impresses visitors today was built 200m (660ft) to the north of the original in about 1277. But why would anyone spend such time, trouble and expense building a second, completely separate castle barely fifty years later? The most convincing explanation, the archaeologists concluded, was that the first had been built too near the salt marsh of the Solway Firth, and became unstable and prone to flooding. (*The location of Caerlaverock is shown on the bottom left-hand corner of the map above*).

The second castle was quite different from its predecessor. It was, uniquely, triangular in plan, with three lofty towers built integrally with the curtain wall, one at each point of the triangle (*see right*). The English writer of the splendid poem *The Roll of Karlaverock*, composed in 1300 to celebrate Edward I of England's successful siege of the fortress, described it perfectly:

'In shape it was like a shield, for it had but three sides round it, with a tower at each corner, but one of them was a double one, so high, so long, and so wide, that the gate was underneath it, well made and strong, with a drawbridge and a sufficiency of other defences … good walls and good ditches filled right up to the brim with water.'

The long and relatively peaceful reigns of the two Alexanders (II and III) that spanned much of the 13th century (1214–86) were looked back on as a golden age by 14th-century Scots who had perforce endured the bitter, bloody and prolonged Wars of Independence with England. The 13th century was certainly a golden age for castle-building in Scotland, as the two castles at Caerlaverock demonstrate.

The 12th century had largely been dominated by castles built of timber and earth. But the years around 1200 saw the advent of the stone castle (*see page 54 for the oldest standing stone castle in Scotland, Castle Sween*). This generally took the form of a strong curtain wall, massively thick and dauntingly high, with defence carried out primarily from the top (the wall head). Typical of this type is the older castle at Caerlaverock. The second, standing castle at Caerlaverock (*see left*) shows just how sophisticated this simple form had become within a generation or so of its appearance. It stands comparison with the greatest castles of this golden age, such as Bothwell (South Lanarkshire), Dirleton (East Lothian) and Kildrummy (Aberdeenshire).

The drawbridge timbers of the second castle (*see right*), discovered in 1962 during archaeological excavation in the inner moat, give us a fascinating insight into the castle's history during that first heady century of occupation. When the timbers were analysed and subsequently dated by tree-ring dating, they showed the original bridge to have been built in the 1270s, undergoing a subsequent repair in the 1330s, and a complete replacement in the 1370s: dates that perfectly mirror the fortunes of Scotland before, during and after the Wars of Independence.

MACLELLAN'S CASTLE

Dumfries and Galloway
Post-Reformation mansion

Right in the heart of the royal burgh of Kirkcudbright, at the point where the Galloway Dee enters the Solway Firth, stands MacLellan's Castle. It wasn't the first castle in the town – that accolade goes to grass-covered Castledykes, on the south fringes of the burgh, established by the Scottish Crown in the 13th century – but it is certainly the one that holds our attention today.

MacLellan's Castle takes its name from its builder, Sir Thomas MacLellan of Bombie (died 1597), scion of a wealthy local family and provost of the town. Sir Thomas grasped the opportunity presented by the Reformation Act of 1560, and within a decade of Scotland becoming a Protestant country he had acquired the church and lands of the former Greyfriars with the intention of knocking down what was left of the friary and building in its stead a fine mansion for himself. Work began in 1570, and was completed within 12 years. The result is one of the largest post-Reformation tower houses to be built. Francis Grose's engraving, published in 1789, shows it from the north, the entrance front (*see right*).

MacLellan's Castle typifies the direction castle-building was taking in the second half of the 16th century. The obsession with closed-up, inward-looking shells was fast giving way to a more open display of conspicuous wealth and comfort. Fortification was not forgotten: the iron yett (gate) at the front entrance is still part of the design, as are the heavy-grilled windows and pistol holes. But these were the late-medieval equivalents of today's outside security lights, door chains and window locks. In an age before banks were invented, people of substance such as Sir Thomas MacLellan had good reason to be concerned about intruders. As a contemporary of Sir Thomas, William Forbes of Corse (Aberdeenshire), allegedly declared in 1581: 'I will build me such a house as thieves will need to knock at ere they enter.'

Builders of post-Reformation tower houses took the quite simple forms that had been handed down to them to new and exciting heights of planning and design. They explored a multiplicity of ground plans, including L-, Z-, E- and T-shaped designs, with many variants of each; they made improvements to the quality of life inside the residence; and they exercised considerable ingenuity in the treatment of exteriors, particularly the wall head (*see right*). The builder of MacLellan's Castle was no exception.

MacLellan's Castle is based on the standard L-plan but with significant variations: an additional tower at one corner, and two more shallow projections in the angle formed around the entrance. Both added to the interest externally, but they also helped to improve arrangements internally, by providing additional stairs to aid circulation (no more would the gentlefolk of the house have to rub shoulders with the servants) and increasing the number of rooms (15 in total, not all of which appear to have been fully fitted out). Another improvement was to the sanitary arrangements, for the builder of MacLellan's dispensed with the draughty open-chute latrines that had served for centuries, and in their place provided closets fitted with 'closed stools' (akin to the modern chemical toilet) that were emptied as required.

Sir Thomas MacLellan's mansion was ready in 1582. Alas, his wife Helen, daughter of Gordon of Lochinvar, had died the previous year, and it was his second spouse Grissel, daughter of another local magnate, Maxwell of Herries, who helped him move in – though she was just 14 years old at the time.

The happy couple enjoyed the delights of their new residence for the next 15 years, raising six children in the process and entertaining the great and good in fine style. In 1587 the guests included King James VI himself, who had lately appointed Sir Thomas a gentleman of the bedchamber (one of the noblemen who attended to the king's dressing arrangements each day). The deserted and roofless castle may look somewhat gaunt and careworn now (*see left*), particularly from St Cuthbert Street, but in its heyday, with its roofscape complete, its outside walls harled over (covered with a gravelly lime plaster), its armorial panels emblazoned with colours, and its surrounding gardens and orchards alive with colour and fragrance, it would have profoundly impressed all who saw it.

As in life, so also in death. At Sir Thomas's passing in 1597, he was laid to rest in the chancel of the old Greyfriars' church. His son and heir, Sir Robert, erected a splendid monument to his father's memory, which can still be seen. One of the finest of Scotland's 'glorious tombs', Sir Thomas's monument, with its columns and pediments, armorial bearings, inscriptions and images (*including Lady Grissel, right*) – not to mention his lordship's recumbent effigy – has stood the test of time rather better than the lord himself.

Cardoness Castle, perched on a small promontory overlooking the estuary of the Water of Fleet, is a prominent landmark for those driving along the A75. Galloway's deeply indented southern coastline is dotted with numerous castles and fortified houses, but Cardoness is perhaps the most outstanding.

In medieval times, Cardoness must have been even more impressive, for then the waters of Fleet Bay lapped against the promontory's base. An English spy, reporting back to Queen Elizabeth

in the 1560s, described how *'Cardines Towre standeth … harde upon the watter of Flete: there can noo ordinance nor gounes endomage yt of the seas, nor there canoo artyllare be taken to it upon the lande … At the ground eb men may ryde under the place upoun the sandes one myle: and at the full sea, boates of eight tonnes may come under the wall.'*

Gradually, though, the waters retreated – just as they did at Caerlaverock (*see page 10*) – and by the time William Daniell visited

CARDONESS CASTLE
Dumfries and Galloway
A tall storey

22

in 1815, it is apparent from his illustration the drama of Cardoness's sea-girt setting had been softened by the 'greening' of the surrounding sands and silts (*see left*). Ten years after Daniell's visit, the local landowner, Alexander Murray of Broughton, had the meandering Water of Fleet canalized to ease the passage of vessels up to the new town of Gatehouse of Fleet. The causeway built in the 1980s to carry the A75 across the Water of Fleet effectively completed Cardoness Castle's isolation from the sea that once helped defend it.

The majority of castles built in 15th-century Scotland took the lofty tower-house form. Cardoness Castle, built about 1475 by the McCullochs, was typical. The rectangular building rose 17m (56ft) to the battlements. Once through the ground-level front door, you were confronted with six floors of accommodation, arranged with storage rooms at the bottom, a fine lord's hall in the middle and private chambers at the top (*see left*).

All six floors and the wall-head battlements were reached by one spiral stair, placed at the corner beside the entrance and corkscrewing its way up through the full height of the building. Clever use was made of the 3m- (10ft-) thick walls to carve out small side chambers at every level. These served a variety of uses, including a guardroom or porter's lodge, a grim two-storey pit-prison, and several closets for use either as bedchambers, wardrobes (store rooms) or latrines.

The most important room in the tower house was the lord's hall on the third floor (*see right*). This is immediately clear from the finely detailed stonework, particularly the fireplace surround, the exquisite aumbry (cupboard) to its left (where the lord's best plate would be displayed), and the pretty stone window seats. However, the elaborate fireplace on the floor above suggests that this level was also of consequence. The cross wall that now divides that level into two was inserted later, but originally it formed one large chamber, the lord's private withdrawing room, where he had his impressive four-poster bed.

The tower house at Cardoness Castle did not stand alone, but had a number of other buildings around it (*see left*). These survive today as reconstructed ruins, making it impossible to determine what functions they served. My guess is that the one immediately beside the front entrance housed the great (outer) hall. The location is identical to the great hall at nearby Threave Castle, the residence of Archibald Douglas 'the Grim', lord of Galloway, who died there in 1400. The hall, the principal reception room in a nobleman's residence, had been at the heart of castle planning from the very outset. It was the setting for all the great occasions – large feasts, gatherings of the household and tenants, and sittings of the baron court. Another building in the castle courtyard would have been the kitchen, for there isn't one in the tower itself. The absence of kitchens within some tower houses has in the past been put down to several factors, the most popular explanations being the fire risk and the undesirable smells. Yet the tower houses of the senior nobility generally did have kitchens, including Archibald the Grim's at Threave. Perhaps a more likely explanation for the lack of kitchens in the tower houses of those a rung or two further down the social ladder, such as the McCullochs, is that with space at a premium, the cooking of private family meals was done over the hall fire, as numerous contemporary woodcuts suggest (*see above*). More public feasts would have been held in a great hall outside, and catered for in an adjacent kitchen. I wonder if any of the 1500 'assorted beasts' stolen in 1505 from a neighbour by Sir Ninian McCulloch was spit-roasted and served up on platters therein.

DUNSKEY CASTLE

Dumfries and Galloway

This house belongs to …

Atop an exposed, rocky spot on the west coast of the Rhinns of Galloway stands grim Dunskey Castle (*see above*). The treacherous waters of the North Channel swirl and roar below, and across the channel the low hills of Antrim in Northern Ireland can faintly be made out. The stronghold has a history as wild as its situation, and in 1489 the murderous McCullochs of Cardoness (*see page 22*) descended on the place, plundered and burnt it as vengeance for the murder of their kinsman by the laird of Dunskey, William Adair. It was probably as a result of this devastation that the Adairs built a new castle on the site, for the oldest part of the present ruin (*see right*) dates to the early years of the 16th century. It was later added to and replanned, probably by Viscount Montgomery, laird of Dunskey from 1608 until his death in 1636, but by 1684 it was already declared 'wholly ruinous'.

Set into the wall directly above the entrance doorway of the tower house are three square stone frames (*see left*). They are empty now, but would originally have held stone plaques carved with coats of arms picked out in bright heraldic colours. To those seeking entry, these conveyed information as to whose house they were visiting. The fashion for putting such stone 'nameplates' on castles dates from the 14th century. Tantallon, the earl of Douglas's castle in East Lothian (*see page 158*), has a simple 'heart' high above its front door, while Robert II's tower house at Dundonald (South Ayrshire) has several heraldic shields proudly displaying the Stewart arms. Gradually these nameplates became more elaborate, incorporating not only the heraldic devices of the lord and lady, but also mottoes, construction dates, and sometimes a pithy epithet. These range from the simple 'WELCVM FRIENDIS' over the front door into Otterston Castle (Fife) to the sobering statement at Drumcoltran Tower (Dumfries and Galloway) advising visitors to 'conceal what is secret; speak little; be truthful; avoid wine; remember death; be merciful'.

As luck has it, we know from other sources that the builder of Dunskey's tower house was William Adair of Kinhilt (died 1513). But had we turned up at his front door five centuries ago, we would not have needed anything else to tell us whose house we were at; the owner's name, standing in society, and perhaps even his social mores, could be deduced just by looking at his nameplate.

GREENAN CASTLE

South Ayrshire
Last in a long line of defence

Greenan Castle clings to its cliff top near the Heads of Ayr as steadfastly as the barnacles do to their rocks on the beach far below. William Daniell illustrates perfectly why this tall, slender tower house has become such a familiar landmark in the views of Ayr Bay (*see above*). Its four internal storeys terminate at the summit in pretty crow-stepped gables and projecting corner turrets, as was very much the fashion when it was built in the early 17th century. Above the ground-floor entrance doorway, the initials 'J K' confirm that this precarious pile was built to house one of the Kennedys, a

powerful Ayrshire clan – probably John Kennedy of Baltersan, a relation of the earl of Cassilis. The date beside the initials, 1603, shows it was among the last tower houses built in Scotland.

John Kennedy was the last in a long line to build defensively on this exposed headland. The Kennedys only acquired Greenan in 1588, from the Davidsons, who had held the barony since at least the 15th century. But long before even they appeared on the scene, Greenan had served as a defended home. A short distance inland from the tower, the remains of four curving, concentric lines were captured on film during aerial reconnaissance in 1978 (*see right*). They are clearly the remains of infilled ditches, and although they have not yet been archaeologically investigated, analogy with similar sites identifies them as being the defences of a promontory fort built in prehistory, well before the Romans invaded. Greenan is far from alone in this respect. At another Ayrshire castle, Dundonald, for example, the hill on which Robert II built his mighty tower house around 1380 was first defended by Bronze-age people over 2000 years earlier.

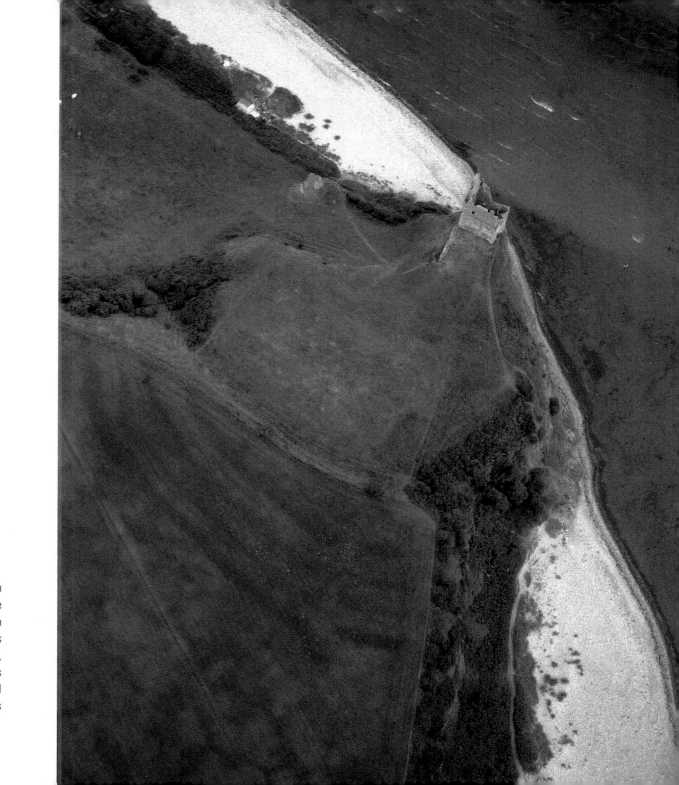

DUMBARTON CASTLE

West Dunbartonshire
Fortress of the Britons

Dumbarton Rock stands guard over the spot where the River Leven joins the River Clyde. It perhaps has a longer recorded history of continuous fortification than any other place in Britain, emerging in the aftermath of the breakdown of Roman rule in the 5th century as the stronghold of the Britons of Strathclyde, and continuing thereafter by turns as a medieval royal castle, as an 18th-century artillery fortress and, finally, as a World War II anti-aircraft battery.

Dumbarton, or *Dun Breatann*, means 'fortress of the Britons', and Dumbarton Rock is everything one imagines the stronghold of a mighty Dark-age warlord to have been. The brute mass of hard volcanic basalt rock rises up almost sheer from the murky depths of the waters that swirl around its base. From its twin peaks (*see photograph on page 36*), White Tower Crag and the Beak, one can see for miles around, northwards over the Vale of Leven to the snow-capped summit of Ben Lomond beyond, westwards down the Clyde

estuary to the mountains of Cowal, southwards across the Clyde to the green Renfrewshire hills, and eastwards, upriver to Glasgow. The Venerable Bede, in the early 8th century, called it *Al Cluith*, 'Clyde Rock', and described it as 'a strongly defended political centre of the Britons', in effect their capital city. It was from here that their powerful kings held sway, sovereigns such as Ceretic, to whom St Patrick wrote around 460 castigating him for raiding a fledgling Christian community in his adopted Ireland; Donald, who ended his days in 975 while on pilgrimage to the 'Eternal City' of Rome; and Duncan, the last to rule, who in 1034 became Duncan I of Scotland. The moment he was enthroned on the Stone of Destiny at Scone was the moment the kingdom of Strathclyde ceased to exist; thereafter Dumbarton Rock was abandoned to the seabirds. Today, all that survives of Dun Breatann, other than the Rock itself, are fragments from two 10th-century stone cross-slabs (*see right*) found on the Rock and now on display in the governor's house.

Dumbarton Castle (*see left*) is first referred to in the foundation charter of the royal burgh of Dumbarton, founded in the shadow of the Rock in 1222.

Clearly, the need for a strong defence had re-emerged, and the cause is not far to seek. In 1098, King Edgar of Scotland, Duncan I's grandson, reluctantly ceded Argyll and the Isles to the king of Norway. (*Edgar's seal, see above, is the earliest representation of a Scottish king.*) Thereafter, an uneasy truce existed between the two countries, creating the conditions for those caught in the middle to play one side off against the other. One local warlord in particular, Somerled — his very name, *sumarlidi* ('summer raider') belies his Viking roots — soon reigned supreme in the Isles, presiding over a 'kingdom' extending from Lorn, in Argyll, to the distant Uists. Such was his power that he even ventured to invade Scotland, audaciously sailing up the Clyde and past Dumbarton Rock in 1164 at the head of an armada of 160 ships. It proved his downfall, for he was killed near Renfrew.

Dumbarton Castle's strategic role as frontier post declined with King Haakon of Norway's ill-fated invasion of 1263 that ended in the débacle at Largs, on the far side of the Clyde estuary, where a large part of Haakon's fleet was lost in a storm. The subsequent treaty of Perth (1266) effectively brought the curtain down on Norway's hegemony in Argyll and the Isles. Thereafter, the royal castle benefited from its relatively secluded position in the land communications of Scotland, being used as a kind of postern gate into and out of the realm. The young David II (in 1334), Princess Margaret, daughter of James I (1435), and – most famously – five-year-old Mary, Queen of Scots (1548) all sailed furtively to France from Dumbarton. The traffic wasn't all one way, and in the turbulent years of the early 16th century, when Scotland and England locked horns once more, John Stewart, duke of Albany and governor of Scotland, invariably used Dumbarton during his various comings and goings. If nothing apart from the Rock survives from Dun Breatann, precious little survives of the medieval castle. What does remain includes the 14th-century portcullis arch, bridging the gap between the twin peaks, and the 16th-century guardhouse below it, both of which appear on an engraving of *c.* 1690 by the Dutch-born military engineer and artist John Slezer (*see right*). But the imposing medieval gatehouse Slezer also depicts was demolished within a few years of his visit to make way for a new artillery defence designed to counter a new threat.

To an extent Dumbarton Castle had long been used by the royal Stewarts as a base from which to control the 'enemy within', most notably the MacDonald lords of the Isles, who were descendants of the mighty Somerled. In 1495, James IV embarked on Admiral Wood's flagship *Flower*, docked at Dumbarton, and sailed to Argyll to oversee the dismembering of the MacDonald power base. In 1689, following the flight into exile of the last Stuart monarch (as the name was by then spelt), James VII of Scotland and II of England, the western Highlands were the prime recruiting ground for the Jacobite army ('Jacobite' is derived from *Jacobus*, Latin for James). Dumbarton, the royal castle closest to the trouble spot, became the focus of renewed attention once more.

In the wake of the 1715 Jacobite Rising, Lieutenant-General George Wade tabled plans for the refortification of the key Scottish royal castles, Dumbarton included. They were put into effect in the 1730s and survive largely intact to this day. The main artillery fortification, King George's Battery, illustrates the painful struggle by the military engineer responsible, Captain John Romer, to adapt an intractable site to contemporary defensive practice. His domed sentinel boxes became something of a Romer trademark (*see left and above*), appearing also at Fort Augustus and the first Fort George, in Inverness (both since demolished) and Edinburgh Castle (*see page 150*). Romer's chiefs need not have worried, for no shot was ever fired in anger from the ramparts – at least so far as we know.

LOCHRANZA CASTLE

Isle of Arran, North Ayrshire
From hall house to tower house

On a narrow tongue of land projecting into Loch Ranza, a sea loch on Arran's north coast, stands lonely Lochranza Castle. It is an unexpectedly fascinating building. Outwardly, it gives the impression of being a typical, late-medieval tower house, with room piled upon room to give that familiar lofty appearance (*see right*). On closer inspection, we find that the tower house has been ingeniously contrived out of a much earlier, more modestly sized medieval structure known as a hall house. Tower houses are relatively commonplace and can be found the length and breadth of Scotland. Hall houses, on the other hand, are few and far between. The reason for this imbalance is not clear. Of course, there is the possibility that many more hall houses were built than now survive. Most may simply have been demolished so that their stone could be reused when the time came for the laird to build afresh, or maybe left to fall into ruin when the site was abandoned. Future excavations will undoubtedly find further examples. The supposedly 7th-century monastery building at St Abb's Head (Scottish Borders), turned out on investigation in 1980 to be a later medieval secular hall. But other hall houses seem simply to have been incorporated into their successors, as at Lochranza. Detecting them, though, is not easy, and the existence of Lochranza's hall house was only first recognized some 40 years ago.

The original L-plan hall house was two storeys high beneath the battlements. The lord's lodging was on the upper floor, above a ground-floor storage area. There were two entrances. Both were formidable obstacles. The one at ground level in the south wall – which might be characterized as the 'tradesman's entrance' – was protected by two doors (one of them probably an iron yett), both protected by sliding draw-bars, and a 'murder hole', or opening in the stone-vaulted ceiling of the small lobby immediately inside, through which the defending garrison could continue to defend the entrance from the safety of the upper floor. The second entrance – the 'front door' – was at a higher level in the east wall (*the blocked opening in the photograph to the left*) and was reached either by a fore stair or ladder that could perhaps have been hauled up and taken inside in the event of trouble. This latter entrance led not directly into the lord's lodging but into a stone stairway that dog-legged up through the building from the ground-floor entrance to the battlements. The stairs had three more barriers along their length, showing how important security was to the lord. (*Plans of the building are shown to the right.*)

So who was the lord? To be truthful, we are not sure. He was probably the same man who built another hall house at Skipness, across the Kilbrannan Sound in Argyll. In 1261, Skipness is known to have been the property of Dougall MacSween, lord of Knapdale, and son of Suibhne (Sven) 'the Red', whose main seat was awesome Castle Sween (*see page 54*) beside the loch of that name. It is tempting to see the two hall houses, at Skipness and Lochranza, providing secure bases for Dougall on either side of the strategic Kilbrannan Sound at a time of growing tension between Scotland and Norway over control of Argyll and the Isles. The MacSweens failed to hold on to their estates in the ensuing showdown that ended with King Haakon of Norway's humiliation at Largs in 1263 and his death shortly after. Arran and Knapdale, with their castles at Lochranza and Skipness, were granted by Alexander III of Scotland to his trusty henchman, Walter Stewart, earl of Menteith.

'front door'

upper floor
(hall and chamber)

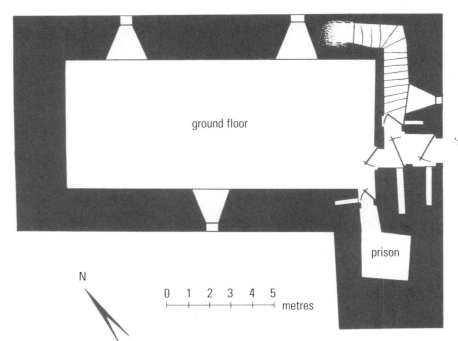

ground floor

'tradesmen's
entrance'

prison

N

0 1 2 3 4 5 metres

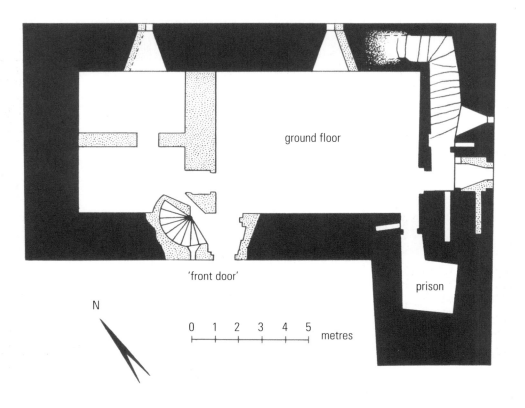

ground floor

'front door'

prison

N

0 1 2 3 4 5 metres

The conversion from hall house to tower house was a single, conscious act, not one that came about by degrees. The original structure was comprehensively remodelled to provide a suitable residence for a nobleman living in James VI's Scotland of the later 16th century. The conversion meant the building was effectively 'turned round'. Whereas the MacSweens had entered from the side overlooking the loch, the new lord had his entrance doorway facing the land. He also planted it firmly at ground level. Evidently, security was still a consideration for the new lord, as the box-machicolation (overhanging parapet with holes in the floor to drop missiles through) at the wall head directly over the doorway demonstrates (*see right*), but this was designed to help warn off undesirables, not to withstand a fully pressed siege. (*The plan of the new ground floor is shown above.*) The identity of the lord who ordered this remodelling is as uncertain as that of the builder of the original hall house, and sadly the armorial panel over the entrance doorway is now empty, leaving no clue as to its previous occupants. However, we know from documentary records that this part of Arran was held by the Montgomery earls of Eglinton throughout the 16th century. It may be significant that the Montgomeries chose to have their castle facing the land for they were truly a Scottish family whose roots were firmly on the mainland; the MacSweens, however, were Islesmen born and bred. We can appreciate that they might wish to look out across the sea to the west, from whence they came.

INVERARAY CASTLE

Argyll and Bute
Campbell's kingdom

Inveraray Castle, beside Loch Fyne, isn't a medieval castle at all but a great 18th-century country seat, designed for Archibald Campbell, 3rd duke of Argyll, by English architect Roger Morris. It was effectively complete by the time of his grace's death in 1761.

The origin of the Campbells (from the Gaelic *Na Caimbeulach*, 'men of the twisted mouths') is obscure, but they had links with the Britons of Strathclyde (*see Dumbarton Castle, page 34*) and even claimed they could trace their roots back to the legendary King Arthur. When Robert the Bruce became king of Scots in 1306, Sir Colin Campbell

possessed a modest land holding beside Loch Awe. By the time of the king's death in 1329, the Campbells, rewarded for their loyal support throughout the Wars of Independence with England, had acquired much of Lorn, Benderloch and Kintyre, most of it from the disgraced MacDougalls of Dunstaffnage (*see page 66*). They became sheriffs of Argyll, then in 1382 its royal lieutenants. The earldom of Argyll followed in 1457, the marquisate in 1641, and the dukedom in 1701. (The portrait seen here is of Archibald, the first marquis, who placed the crown of Scotland on Charles II's head at Scone in 1651 but who was executed ten years later for rising up against him).

Inveraray had been the chief seat of Clan Campbell since the day in 1457 when James II created another Sir Colin Campbell earl of Argyll. Sir Colin marked his elevation by moving the ancestral home from Innis Chonnell, on neighbouring Loch Awe, to the place where the River Aray enters the northern shore of Loch Fyne. (*The view here looks down onto Inveraray from the towered folly on top of Dun na Cuaiche*). There Colin built a great tower house, and there for the next three hundred years resided in succession the earls, marquises and dukes of Argyll, at least on those occasions they spent in the Highlands.

In due course, the earls found the great tower house too cramped, and one of their number in the later 16th century had a wing added to the original rectangular tower, so converting it into an L-plan and freeing up valuable space in the process. Additional ranges were subsequently built in the courtyard. But then cracks began to appear in the 'old tour', and it was noticed that the building was in danger of slipping down into the Aray. The decision was therefore taken to rebuild anew close by. Once Roger Morris's new Gothic pile was ready, the old tower was demolished in its entirety, so William Daniell arrived 40 years too late to sketch it. However, a previous visitor, the artist John Clerk of Eldin, captured images of both ducal seats in the brief time they were standing together in the 1760s. Today the spot where the ancient castle stood is marked by three humble concrete pillars.

Inveraray Castle's location – well inland but on a sea loch – confirms the crucial role water played in 'Campbell's kingdom'; it was so important that the Campbells incorporated a ship, the galley of Lorn, into their coat of arms (*see above*). The water wasn't necessarily seawater, though, for in the Campbell's formative years landlocked Loch Awe lay at the heart of their world. Their former *caput*, or chief seat, before the move to Inveraray was the island stronghold of Innis Chonnell, at the southern end of Loch Awe. It is now an ivy-clad ruin that may originally have been similar to Castle Sween (*see page 54*) in both date and form. Another Campbell castle, Kilchurn (*see left*),

guarded the north end of Loch Awe. So important had the Campbells become by the 15th century, and so extensive their lands, that in order for them to maintain control the family had to split into various branches, known as *sliochdan*, each under its own chief but ultimately answerable to the clan chief. The powerfully impressive castle of Kilchurn was built around 1450 by another Sir Colin Campbell after he was entrusted with the lordship of Glenorchy by his nephew, the first earl. Thereafter, Kilchurn served as the chief seat of the Campbells of Glenorchy, who in time acquired almost as much land and power as the senior Campbell line.

CASTLE SWEEN
Argyll and Bute
Scotland's oldest-standing castle

Near the southern end of Loch Sween, in close proximity to its junction with the Sound of Jura, crouches Castle Sween on its rocky ridge. This ancient and remarkable fortress dates from the end of the 12th century, and has the distinction of being Scotland's oldest-standing stone castle. The builder was Suibhne (Sven) 'the Red', a man of both Gaelic and Norse blood and the progenitor of Clan MacSween.

The sea was in the blood of the Gaels from the time they arrived in Argyll early in the first millennium AD. More than a millennium later, their descendants were still depicting themselves on grave slabs with sailed and oared galleys, called *birlinns*, as the memorial on Iona of Bricius MacKinnon (*see right*) shows. Suibhne himself was lord of a largely maritime lordship encompassing lands and lochs across a wide sweep of Knapdale, Kintyre and the Firth of Clyde (*see*

Lochranza Castle, page 42). Even after they were ousted from their territories by the kings of Scots in the later 13th century, they returned with their fleets time and again, and a celebrated Gaelic poem from about 1300 waxes lyrical about John MacSween returning to 'a pleasant anchorage in the bosom of Knapdale' determined to reclaim his birthright, perhaps a reference to the head of Loch Sween, in the Tayvallich area, which Daniell chose for his viewpoint (*left*).

Castles first appeared in Scotland in the 12th century. They were introduced not just by one foreign element, the Normans, but also by their non-feudal, non-Latinized kinsmen, the Norsemen; for Norse *jarls* (or earls) had controlled much of the north and west of Scotland, chiefly Shetland, Orkney, Caithness, Argyll and the Isles since the Vikings appeared on the scene around 800. The first castles were built largely of timber, and relied heavily on earthworks for their defence; the Norman word *motta*, from which we get 'motte', literally means 'clod of earth'. Where stone was used, it was normally restricted to church buildings, such as St Margaret's Chapel in Edinburgh Castle, built around 1130 (*see page 150*), or used solely as a foundation material. The exception was Orkney and Caithness, where the remains of remarkably early stone keeps still exist, including Cubbie Roo's Castle (Orkney), built around 1145 (*see page 112*). The reason is not hard to find, for the Northern Isles were blessed with excellent building stone but almost entirely devoid of trees. Stone as a building material for castles elsewhere emerges only as the 12th century draws to its close. Lost amid the clutter of later medieval buildings at Aberdour Castle (Fife) is the stump of a stone keep that, judging by its double-lancet window, cubical masonry and pilaster at one corner, must date from before 1200. But nowhere else in medieval Scotland proper is there a rival to Aberdour, and we have to cross to the western seaboard, that twilight world caught culturally between Scotland and Norway, to discover the country's best-preserved, oldest-standing castle — Castle Sween (*see left*).

Sween shares common features with Aberdour, most noticeably those conspicuous pilasters; here they clasp not just the corners, but the midpoints along the walls, and envelop the entrance gateway as well (*see right*). But there the similarity with Aberdour stops. Sween is no stone keep but a formidable enclosure-castle, with curtain walls 2m (6.5ft) thick protecting an area roughly the size of two tennis courts. What Suibhne had in that enclosure in the way of buildings is far from clear, for during the course of the 13th century substantial alterations and additions were made to the whole place. These included raising or rebuilding the wall heads, and adding an extension to the west overlooking the loch. Notwithstanding these changes, Sween remains a most remarkable castle, and Suibhne himself seems to have been a remarkable man. Not only did he found a clan, he inspired other clan chiefs to follow his lead in castle-building – MacLean at Duart, MacDougall at Dunstaffnage, MacDonald at Mingary, MacRuari at Tioram and others. These castles of the western seaboard are quite extraordinary strongholds. Here in Argyll and the Isles, far beyond the influence of the Normans, rose some of the most impressive castles built in the 13th century, rivalling anything being constructed in the realm of the Scottish kings. Yet Suibhne and his peers were not feudal aristocrats of Norman stock but chiefs of mixed Gaelic and Viking parentage. What possessed them to build as they did will forever remain a mystery, but our legacy of castles is the richer for their efforts.

DUNOLLIE CASTLE

Argyll and Bute
Power centre of Dalriada

Ivy-clad Dunollie Castle stands upon a rocky shelf commanding magnificent views of the narrow sea channel into Oban Bay and the Firth of Lorn beyond (*see right*). Daniell captures the drama of its situation wonderfully (*see above*). It is not hard to appreciate why this location served as a place of defence for well over a thousand years. The prefix *dun* – the ancient Gaelic word for 'fort' – shows that this was a fortified spot from early times. Fortified places with

names incorporating *dun* abound throughout Scotland. They include pivotal tribal centres such as Dumbarton (*Dun Breatann* – 'fort of the Britons') and Dunkeld ('fort of the Caledonians').

Dunollie likewise was of major importance, as a power centre of Dalriada, the kingdom established in Argyll by a Gaelic-speaking tribe from Ireland, the Dál Riata.

The story goes that the Gaels of Dál Riata, under their legendary leader Fergus Mór (literally, 'Big Fergus'), crossed the treacherous North Channel from the glens of Antrim to the rocky coast of Argyll around the year 500. In reality, they had probably infiltrated well before then, and Big Fergus may simply have been the first member of their royal family to rule from the British side of the Irish Sea. The Romans called these invaders from Ireland *Scotti*. The name may simply mean 'pirates'; they called themselves Gaels (*Goidil* in Old Irish), and the very name 'Argyll' comes from the Gaelic *Earra Ghaidheal*, 'coastland of the Gaels'.

The Dál Riata were organized into kindreds, or extended families, called *cenéla*. Their Argyll lands were divided between three *cenéla*, Loairn, nGabhráin and nOengus, each named after its founder. Cenél Loairn inhabited northern Argyll, including what is now Lorn, and

Dunollie (*see left*) was the imposing fort from where their kings ruled. Very little is known about Dunollie's history, though we know that the Irish enemies of cenél Loairn sacked it in 698, and that Selbach, king of cenél Loairn, had it rebuilt shortly after. Scarcely a trace of ancient Dunollie is visible today, though excavations in 1978 uncovered remains of a rampart skirting the landward side.

Dunollie invites comparison with another Dalriadan power centre, Dunadd, 37km (23 miles) to its south and seat of cenél nGabhráin. Dunadd never had a later medieval castle built on it, and we can see how that rocky hill has been carefully engineered to create a hierarchy of spaces, a design Dunollie might well have mirrored. And near Dunadd's summit are features that Dunollie might also have shared: footprints hollowed out of the bedrock (*see above*), most likely used during the inauguration ceremony for a new king.

Dunollie Castle itself was built long after the ancient power centre of Dalriada there had been abandoned in the late 1st millennium. In fact, the site may not have been refortified until the 15th century, the most likely date for the four-storey tower house that today dominates the rocky shelf (*see left*). The builder was a MacDougall, a clan that traced its lineage back through Dubhgall (Dougall), its eponymous founder, to Somerled 'king of the Isles' (died 1164). We shall encounter Dougall of Lorn at our next castle, Dunstaffnage.

The lordship of Lorn passed by marriage to a branch of the ubiquitous Stewarts in 1388, when the male MacDougall line ended. The position of clan chief passed to a cousin, Ian, the 7th lord of Dunollie. It may have been this up-turn in the MacDougall of Dunollie's fortunes that inspired the building of a new stone castle on the site. The jury is still out as to whether any of the existing complex predates the 15th century, but the probability is that the tower house and adjacent courtyard wall were built together. One intriguing feature in the tower points to a continuing link with Ireland: the basement vaulting was built using wickerwork shuttering, a technique commonly found in the Emerald Isle but only found in Scotland at Dunollie Castle and at Castle Tioram, in Moidart (Highland).

Three centuries after building Dunollie Castle, the MacDougalls forsook their ancient rocky perch for a somewhat austere Georgian house down in the lee of the dun, leaving the castle walls to continue to withstand the battering winds and rains (*see right*).

DUNSTAFFNAGE CASTLE

Argyll and Bute

Stronghold of the son of Somerled

Dunstaffnage Castle stands at the point where Loch Etive and the Firth of Lorn meet. The tongue of land on which it stands is now shrouded in trees, making it hard for today's visitor to appreciate the strategic siting of the ancient stronghold. When Daniell visited, he found only saplings, and his view (*see above*) illustrates just how powerfully impressive and perfectly positioned the castle was in former times.

Dunstaffnage, the chief seat of Clan MacDougall, guarded the seaward approach from the firth via Loch Etire and the Pass of Brander into the heart of Scotland. When it was built around 1220, Argyll lay on the frontier between the kingdoms of Scotland and Norway. In reality, though, neither king directly controlled the region. Instead, the sons of Somerled, 'king of the Isles', a man of mixed Gaelic and Norse parentage, took over their father's patrimony upon his death in 1164. The eldest, Dubhgall (Dougall), claimed his father's power base of Lorn, ruling over most of Argyll as well as the islands of Mull, Lismore, Kerrera, Scarba, Jura, Coll and Tiree. It was his son, Duncan MacDougall, Somerled's grandson, who built Dunstaffnage Castle. The discovery in the castle of a 'king' piece from a medieval chess-set (*see right*) nicely underlines this MacDougall regality.

Sir Duncan MacDougall, contrary to what one might believe, was no 'small time' petty chief operating on the very fringe of the known world; he was a powerful lord, with large forces and fleets at his disposal, who wielded significant political clout. He moved easily between the two realms competing for his loyalty. At one point (1230) he was leading the successful Norse attack on Rothesay Castle, the high steward of Scotland's stronghold on Bute; but later (1237) he was travelling to Rome as the king of Scots' ambassador. Perhaps the site of newly built Rothesay inspired Duncan to construct Dunstaffnage, for the latter's stone curtain wall is simply Rothesay's circular curtain adapted to a more difficult site.

The curtain wall rises up sheer from the plug of rock on which it sits (*see photograph on page 71*). It is massive, over 3.5m (11ft) thick, and almost entirely featureless, with just the occasional narrow lancet window (later blocked up) high up in the wall and small drainage outlets at the base. (The two projecting round towers and the gatehouse entrance were not part of the original scheme.) Whatever went on in the way of courtly life took place behind firmly closed doors. Outwardly, Duncan's stronghold was no welcoming sight (*see left*).

How strange then that the same man should have built a very different structure within bow shot of his awesome residence. The castle chapel, now hidden from view in the trees but prominently depicted in Griffiths's 18th-century engraving as it was meant to be seen (*right*), is an attractive and sophisticated structure. Together with the little priory church Duncan built at Ardchattan, beside Loch Etive 10km (6 miles) east of Dunstaffnage, it hints at a very different personality from the one holed up in the castle.

Dunstaffnage's affinity with Rothesay continued through the century. Around 1260, Rothesay's simple, circular curtain wall had circular towers grafted on to it. These projected boldly out from the wall, increasing the castle's defensive capability by allowing defenders to shoot their arrows along the length of the wall instead of being restricted to shooting down from the top. The towers also provided Rothesay's Stewart lord with additional accommodation. A similar thing happened at Dunstaffnage, under Duncan's son Ewen who inherited the lordship of Lorn in the 1240s, though the towers are not as prominent due to the constraints of the rocky plug. Ewen inherited not only the lordship but his father's and grandfather's cunning. Initially throwing in his lot with Haakon IV of Norway, he became 'king' over all the isles from Man to Lewis. He then transferred his allegiance to Alexander III of Scotland before Haakon's doomed invasion of 1263. It proved a shrewd move and Ewen was soon lording it over all of Argyll on behalf of his new royal master. We can easily see Ewen marking his elevated status by adding those projecting round towers to the curtain wall. They were fitted with the latest military technology: tall, slender shovel-shaped arrow slits (*see left*) for use by soldiers armed with longbows.

Ewen was succeeded by his son Alexander, whose very name reflects the new political reality in the west. But unlike his father, Alexander MacDougall backed the wrong horse during the Wars of Independence that followed Edward I of England's invasion in 1296, throwing in his lot with the English against Robert Bruce. By the summer of 1308, the forces of MacDougall and Bruce confronted each other at the Pass of Brander, on the lower slopes of Ben Cruachan overlooking Loch Etive. Bruce won, and the MacDougalls' defeat effectively marked the end of their hold on power in the west. The stronghold of the son of Somerled was now the property of the king of Scots.

AROS CASTLE

Isle of Mull, Argyll and Bute
Seat of the lord of the Isles

Alone on a hill on the northeast coast of Mull, looking out over the Sound of Mull towards the mainland, is Aros Castle; Daniell captures its solitude wonderfully (*see above*). It is a modest ruin belying a far from modest past, for 'Dounearwyse' (Dun Aros) was once a principal seat of the mighty MacDonalds, lords of the Isles. Aros wasn't built by them – that honour is claimed by the MacDougalls of Lorn, lords of Dunstaffnage, in the 13th century – but following the MacDougalls' showdown with Robert I (the Bruce)

in 1308 and their subsequent downfall, the MacDonalds, descended from Somerled's grandson, Donald, Dougall's nephew, acquired Aros and very much made it their home.

Not every MacDonald threw in his lot with the Bruce, but Angus Og MacDonald of Islay did, helping the king to his sensational victory over the English at Bannockburn in 1314. Angus and his son John soon reaped their reward, receiving extensive lands from Kintyre to

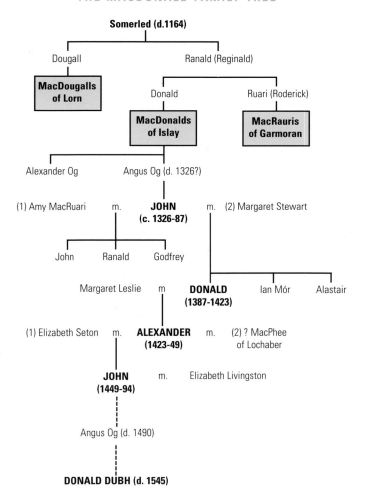

Lochaber, including Mull. And when in 1346 John married Amy MacRuari, sole heir of the last chief of Clan MacRuari, and acquired all the remaining Hebridean islands save Skye, it was as if Somerled's former dominion had been resurrected (Ruari was Donald's younger brother). John MacDonald now styled himself *Dominus Insularum*, 'lord of the Isles'. Donald (died 1423), the second lord, and John (died 1494), the fourth lord, both issued edicts while in residence at Aros. The MacDonald family tree is seen right.

73

Aros Castle is what we today call a hall house, to distinguish the type from the more lofty tower house (*see above*). Hall houses were just two storeys high beneath the battlements, with the lord's hall taking up most of the upper floor – hence the generic name. The unvaulted undercroft at ground level probably served as storage space. We saw a similar hall house earlier at Lochranza (*see page 42*) – similar, that is, both in date (13th century) and in size – Aros is 25 x 13m (82 x 43ft), and Lochranza is 21 x 11m (69 x 36ft).

Hall houses weren't the sum total of the castle accommodation, of course, but simply the heart of a larger complex of structures that together comprised the lordly seat. At Aros, a cluster of less substantial buildings surrounds the hall house (*left*). All that remain of these today are grass-covered humps and bumps, and as none of them has yet been excavated we can say little about them. But a visit to the MacDonalds' ancestral seat of Finlaggan, on Islay, helps us to envisage how impressive such superficially modest lordly residences could be. The Finlaggan complex sprawls over two islands, linked by a causeway. The larger Eilean Mór ('big island') contains more than twenty structures alone. One at least housed the hall, and another served as the chapel. Medieval castles didn't necessarily need mighty curtain walls or tall tower houses to make them imposing.

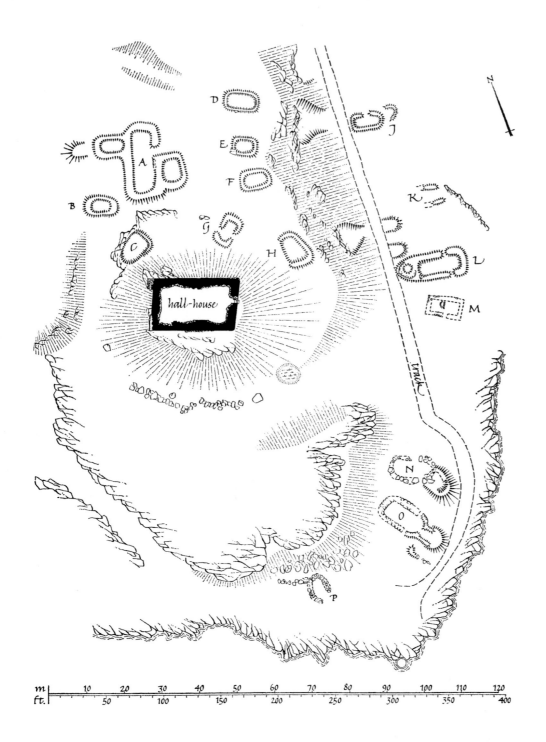

hall-house

Across the Sound of Mull, within sight of Aros, sits another modest hall-house castle, Ardtornish, the ground plan (*left*) and view (*right*) of which are included here. The two castles could be peas from the same pod. Ardtornish's hall house is much the same size as Aros – 23 x 15m (75 x 49ft) – and is likewise surrounded by less-substantial structures. The only significant difference is the apparent lack of a defensive ditch on Ardtornish's landward side. Like Aros, Ardtornish probably wasn't built by the MacDonalds, but acquired from the MacRuaris when John and Amy tied the knot in 1346.

The hall houses at Aros and Ardtornish weren't modest homes, but focal points of larger, hierarchical complexes of structures and spaces, as would be appropriate to the nature of baronial privilege and obligation, and which reflect the scale and complexity of their large households. When we see their now-tumbledown ruins in this light, we begin to appreciate why in 1462 commissioners representing Edward IV of England felt able to come to Ardtornish to negotiate with Sir John MacDonald, the fourth lord of the Isles, the famous political alliance known as the treaty of Ardtornish-Westminster. That pact led directly to the confrontation between the king of Scots and the lord of the Isles, and by the end of the 15th century to the downfall of the mighty lords. Aros, Ardtornish and Finlaggan passed to other lesser lords, and their great days as seats of the lords of the Isles were over.

MINGARY CASTLE

Highland
Hebridean bolt-hole

Mighty Mingary, on the Ardnamurchan peninsula, stands comparison with the other formidable 13th-century, curtain-walled castles of the west, such as Dunstaffnage (*see page 66*). The views from its battlements are simply stunning: westwards to the ocean, southwards across the Sound of Mull, and eastwards inland up Loch Sunart. Just as at Dunstaffnage, one can readily appreciate why Mingary is where it is. The telltale signs that Mingary is 13th-century in origin are there: the high, thick and irregular curtain wall hugging its rocky perch, and the almost complete absence of openings in that wall, just the odd narrow lancet window (*see right*). But which grandson of Somerled actually built this stronghold just 10km (6 miles) from the westernmost tip of the British mainland – Ruari or Donald? And when in the 14th century did it pass to the Maclans of Ardnamurchan? Perhaps we shall never know. However, it is what became of it later in its career as a Hebridean bolt-hole that makes it important.

Mingary Castle isn't actually mentioned in any record until 1495, when James IV arrived in person, aboard the warship *Flower*, to ensure compliance with his recent decree declaring the MacDonald lord of the Isles forfeit and his former dominions annexed to the crown. MacIan of Ardnamurchan had made his peace with the king the previous year, and demonstrated his loyalty by orchestrating MacDonald's delivery into royal captivity. This first mention of Mingary was certainly not its last. For the next 250 years the ancient stronghold repeatedly figured in the turbulent civil history of early-modern Scotland.

In the early 1500s, Mingary was caught in the crossfire between the warring MacIans and MacDonalds, then later in the century in the bitter feud between the MacIans and the MacLeans of Duart. A bizarre episode took place in 1588, when MacLean laid siege to Mingary, ably assisted by Spanish troops recently rescued from their Armada galleon, which had taken refuge in Tobermory Bay! Even with this extra support, the siege proved unsuccessful, though it did prompt MacIan to reconstruct the curtain wall's upper defences. The wall head facing the land was heightened by 2m (6ft), the original crenelles (notched parapet) were converted into gunholes, and a new wooden hoarding, or battlement, was fitted to oversail the curtain wall, enabling the garrison to cover the ground directly beneath (*see right*). The seaward wall heads were upgraded too, including the addition of round turrets to the two corners. The presence of such formidable defences explains the difficulty the MacDonalds had in capturing the castle in 1644, during the Civil War — even though the Macdonalds came armed with cannon such as the one found lying on the beach below the castle

(*see above*). The contemporary account is fascinating — and very revealing about the process of siege and counter-siege:

'He [Alasdair MacDonald] forced the strong castle by a desperate assault … for they had neither cannon to batter nor pittard to blow up, nor scaled ladders to ascend the walls, and yet, notwithstanding the incessant showers of musket balls that came from the walls, with the continual playing of their other ordnance, they regarded it no more than if they had been snowballs; marching and advancing speedily till they were at the foot of the wall, then firing the gates and heaping all sorts of combustible stuff round about, they set fire to the castle, maintaining the fuel till they within were almost choked; and to add more malour [misfortune] to those confounded defenders, the continual thundering of musket and cannon did so shake the rock as their well went dry, and having some puncheons of ale, they are forced to pour them down above the gate where they were most infested with fire; at length, finding no end of their enemy's assault night nor day, thirst, watching and weariness forced them to yield.'

By the time of the 1644 siege, MacIan of Ardnamurchan's castle and lands had been swallowed up by the powerful Campbell earls of Argyll. Following the overthrow in 1689 of the Catholic James VII and II, the last Stuart monarch, by the Protestant William and Mary, major rebuilding works were carried out inside Mingary's giant stone shell. Either Archibald, the tenth earl, or Sir Alexander Campbell of Lochnell, to whom Archibald entrusted the castle and lands in 1696, could have been responsible.

There is some doubt as to whether the range built along the landward side of the ancient curtain (*see left*) was meant for lordly use. My guess is that it was not. The three-storey plus attic building has more the feel of soldiers' barracks than noble residence. Each floor has the same layout (a large and a small room either side of a central straight stair) and the courtyard windows are similarly symmetrical (*see right*). There is no hierarchy in either space or

design such as one would expect in a lordly house of the period. The building has more in common with the barracks built inside another Campbell castle, Kilchurn (*see page 52*), around the same time. Assuming 12 men to each larger room, with their officers and NCOs in the smaller rooms, we have accommodation for a company of foot soldiers (around 60 men).

No surprise then to discover 59 officers and men billeted at Mingary in January 1746. These were redcoats out-stationed from Fort William, government troops fighting for George II against Prince Charles Edward Stuart's Jacobite army. 'Bonnie Prince Charlie' had first set foot on the British mainland not far from Mingary in August 1745, and the Campbells had quickly dispatched a small detachment of troops there to help patrol the area. This was what Mingary was good for, holding a small garrison in relative safety and capable of being supplied from the sea – a Hebridean bolt-hole, in fact.

EILEAN DONAN CASTLE

Highland
Phoenix from the flames

'Saint Donan's isle', situated where lochs Alsh, Duich and Long meet, has a far from saintly past.

Here at this ancient stronghold of the Mackenzies of Kintail, in 1331, Thomas Randolph, earl of Moray and guardian of Scotland for the infant David II, had the castle walls 'decorated' with the heads of 50 Highlanders. They were peremptorily executed to serve as a warning to those who might be tempted to take the opportunity presented by King Robert the Bruce's death to rebel – the region had after all only been free of Norwegian rule those past 60 years, and some had not forgotten the old loyalties.

In 1539, Donald Gorm MacDonald of Sleat, who resided at Dun Sgathaich on Skye, feuded with the Mackenzies and was killed attacking the castle; the arrow that fatally wounded him was allegedly the last one left in the defenders' armoury.

At the start of the Jacobite Rising of March to June 1719, the ageing castle was garrisoned for the final time by some 300 Spanish soldiers fighting for the exiled James VIII and III, the 'Old Pretender'. Early on the morning of 10 May, two Royal Navy warships, the *Worcester* and the *Enterprise*, sailed up Loch Alsh, dropped anchor off the island and began to bombard the castle. The terrified garrison, unable to resist the onslaught, withdrew from the castle, enabling a landing party to go ashore, lay mines in the powder magazine and blow the place to smithereens. (The Jacobites were routed shortly after in nearby Glen Shiel.) And that is what Daniell found a century later – a ruin (*see left*).

And thus it remained until Lieutenant-Colonel MacRae-Gilstrap, descended from the hereditary keepers of Eilean Donan, restored it between 1912 and 1932, unveiling a phoenix from the flames and now Scotland's most photographed castle (*see above*).

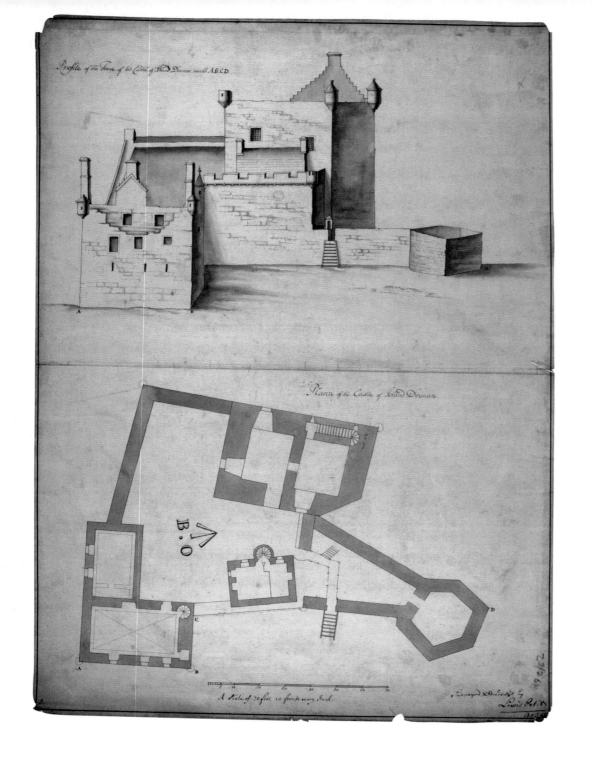

Profile of the Front of the Castle of Island Dounan mark'd A B C D

Plann of the Castle of Island Dounan

B : O

A Scale of 70 feet 10 foot to every Inch

Surveyed & Delineated by
Lewis Petit

The restoration of Eilean Donan owes more to Victorian Romantic medievalism than to sound research; indeed, MacRae-Gilstrap claimed that the castle's 'original' appearance had been revealed to him in a dream! It certainly wasn't revealed through the detailed survey of the castle made by Brigadier-General Petit in 1714, just five years before it was blown up, for that did not come to light until shortly before the 'restoration' ended. Lewis Petit, a military engineer with a distinguished service record in Spain and Portugal, had been sent to Scotland by the Board of Ordnance (BO), the government body responsible for all military building and provisioning, to record strongholds likely to be capable of use by the army during another Jacobite uprising. His survey shows the castle complex as he found it: all the buildings were unroofed save the one immediately beside the simple entrance (*see left*). More significantly, perhaps, he records no fancy three-arched bridge linking the island castle to the shore.

CANDIDE FORTITUDINE

SECURE

1912

NEC·CURO·NEC·CAREO

CHO FAD'S A BHIOS MACRATH A STIGH
CHA BHI FRISEALACH A MUIGH.

JM'RG
1928

EM'RG
1928

CAISTEAL MAOL

Isle of Skye, Highland
Castles and brochs

Caisteal Maol ('the bare castle' in Gaelic), is one of Scotland's most familiar landmarks but one of its least-familiar castles. The ruined stump, looking for all the world like a badly decayed tooth, stands beside Kyleakin, on the coast of Skye, near to where the ferryboat to Kyle of Lochalsh formerly berthed and now the road bridge passes (*right*). The castle thus guarded one of the most strategic positions in the Hebrides, the narrow strait of Kyle Akin (Kyle is derived from the Gaelic *caol*, meaning 'narrows') separating Skye from the mainland. It was through here that King Haakon IV of Norway sailed in the late summer of 1263 on route to his date with destiny at the battle of Largs; Kyle Akin literally means 'Haakon's Narrows'.

Caisteal Maol was known as Dunakin ('fort of Haakon') in medieval times, but the ruin that teeters on the brink today is no older than the 15th century. It comprised a plain, rectangular tower house, three storeys high, with insufficient space around it for other buildings. Curiously, a hoard of 70 coins, dating from the later 16th century, was found there in 1951, hidden in a chink of masonry in the west wall. In the Scotland of James VI, Dunakin was the seat of the MacKinnons. But early in the following century they moved to Kilmarie, in the shadow of the Cuillin Hills. In a way, the MacKinnon chief was simply returning to his ancestral roots, for the original clan seat had been at Dun Ringill, just a stone's throw away from Kilmarie beside Loch Slapin.

Dun Ringill (*see above*) isn't a castle but a two-thousand-year-old Iron-age structure refortified and reoccupied by the MacKinnons around a thousand years later. The dun is typical of these later prehistoric defended sites. A near-circular, thick-walled, dry-stone structure with one very narrow entrance passage complete with door-checks and drawbar-slots, and one mural cell. However, two features betray the fact that this ancient fortress was still serving as a stronghold in the medieval period: a ditch around the outside, and the foundations of two rectangular buildings within.

Dun Ringill may well be more representative of the fortified residences of those holding maritime lordships across the western seaboard in the 12th and 13th centuries than we assume. Our eyes are drawn to

the likes of Sween (*see page 54*) and Dunstaffnage (*see page 66*) because they are impressive, but they may be the exceptions.

The fact that many castle sites have the prefix *dun* suggests a continuity of fortified settlement of which the medieval castle was the last in the sequence. Archaeological excavation has shown how some Iron-age duns continued as fortified residences long into the Middle Ages. And when we gaze upon those few prehistoric broch towers standing almost to their full height, such as Dun Telve, Glenelg, directly opposite Skye and the most complete broch on the Scottish mainland (*see right*), we can see a certain similarity with medieval tower houses, and understand why books on Scottish castles often begin with brochs.

DUNVEGAN CASTLE
Isle of Skye, Highland
The longest continuously occupied house in Scotland

At the head of Loch Dunvegan stands Dunvegan Castle, clan seat of the MacLeod chiefs since the early 13th century and still lived in by them. This makes Dunvegan the longest continuously occupied house in Scotland.

The oldest parts – the much-reconstructed seaward-facing curtain wall and sea gate – were built by Leod himself, who lorded it over northern Skye and the Outer Hebrides under the watchful eye of his king, Haakon IV of Norway (*see also Bishop's Palace, Kirkwall, page 96*). Down the centuries other parts were added to his stronghold, notably the great tower (to the right of the main entrance) some time in the 14th century, and the 'Fairy Tower' (to the left of the main entrance) by Alasdair Crotach MacLeod (died 1547), the eighth chief. 'Hunchbacked Alasdair' (*crotach* means 'the bent') also built a splendid tomb for himself in St Clement's Church (*Tur Chliamainn*), at Rodel, across the Minch on Harris, the mountains of which are visible from Dunvegan and which Daniell depicts in his view (*see above*); the tomb's wonderful decoration (*see right*) includes a depiction of a castle, most probably Dunvegan. More tinkering with the castle followed in the 17th century, particularly by Rory Mór ('big Rory') and Iain Breac ('spotty') MacLeod.

By the time of Ian Breac MacLeod's death in 1693, the temptation to leave the exposed rocky plateau on which Dunvegan stands must have been hard to resist. Perhaps the family might well have done so had Dr Johnson not stayed with Lord and Lady MacLeod in 1773 during his tour of the Hebrides. Johnson's wonderfully persuasive argument for staying put was recorded for posterity by his travelling companion, James Boswell:

'Lady MacLeod insisted that the rock was very inconvenient. That there was no place near where a good garden could be made; that it would always be a rude place; that it was a Herculean labour to make a dinner here; that the climate was such that one might have half an hour fair now and then, though it rained in general. "Madam, (said I), if once you quit this rock, this centre of gravity, there is no knowing where you may settle. No, no; keep to the rock: it is the very jewel of the estate. It looks as if it had been let down from heaven by the four corners, to be the residence of a chief. Have all the comforts and conveniences of life upon it, but never leave Rorie Mor's cascade."'

Lord and Lady MacLeod did indeed stay put. Furthermore, in 1790 they invited the architect Walter Boak to convert the decrepit medieval castle into a castellated 'modern' mansion (*see left and above*). Over the next fifty years and more, some parts were taken down and other parts heightened, larger windows were put in and mock embattled parapets put on. Perhaps the most significant change to the castle was the creation of a new, much grander, main entrance facing the land (*see above*).

This glorious confection – essentially a 19th-century country house in medieval dress – is what welcomes visitors today, as they arrive at the front door in their thousands. A far cry from how things looked in Leod's day. For one thing, there would have been no front door facing the land; visitors in ancient times would normally have arrived at the old sea gate, by boat. This complete about-face says much about the changing world of the Hebridean nobleman from medieval to modern times. Where formerly the MacLeod chiefs had cherished the view westwards to the open sea whence their ancestors had arrived, by the time of Johnson and Boswell's visit they were appreciating the delights on offer far to the east, in Edinburgh, London, even Paris. No more would they be rowed up Loch Dunvegan in their oared galley; from now on they would arrive by land in a pony and trap.

BISHOP'S PALACE, KIRKWALL

Orkney

'Where the Norwayen banners flout the sky'

Kirkwall is the capital of Orkney. For centuries it was the capital of the Norse-held *Nordreyjar* – Orkney and Shetland. But that ended in 1469 when Christian I of Norway failed to pay the dowry promised to his son-in-law, James III of Scotland, and James called in the debt by assuming sovereignty of the Northern Isles.

Kirkwall stands at the edge of the Bay of Kirkwall; the Norwegians called it *Kirkjugvar*, 'church bay', and one glance at Daniell's painting (*see above*) is sufficient to see why. The great mass of St Magnus's Cathedral (*see right*) dominated then, as it did from its beginning in the 12th century, and as it continues to do today.

Kirkwall is the most northerly cathedral city in Britain, though when St Magnus's was built the inhabitants belonged to the archdiocese of Trondheim, not St Andrews.

Kirkwall was graced in former times by three fortified noble residences. The only one actually called a castle was Kirkwall Castle, stronghold of the Sinclair earls of Orkney from the late 14th century; built between the cathedral and the bay, it was demolished around 1615. The other two, however – the Bishop's Palace and Earl's Palace – do survive, and they are among the most fascinating ancient buildings in all Scotland.

The Bishop's Palace was built around the same time as St Magnus's Cathedral to provide a suitably dignified residence for the prelate. It was just a stone's throw from the cathedral's south transept (*see left*). The first to reside there may well have been Bishop William 'the Old' (died 1168), coped crusader and friend of Earl Rognvald, St Magnus's nephew and patron of the cathedral. The ancient episcopal residence has a long and chequered history, and what remains today is bewildering. But analysing the architecture reveals clues in the masory. Peel away the later alterations and additions and one is left with a two-storey hall house, not unlike those at Lochranza and Aros (*pages 42 and 72*), but differently proportioned – the Bishop's Palace, 28 x 8m (92 x 26ft), is longer and thinner. Little of the original first-floor hall survives, but at ground-floor level in the west wall are eight narrow windows that clearly belong to the 12th century; the internal openings are all built of stones alternating in colour between red and yellow, just as in the cathedral itself.

Within this building on 15 December 1263 died Haakon IV, the last king of Norway to rule over the *Sudreyjar*, the 'southern Isles' of Argyll and the Hebrides. All noble castles and episcopal palaces, royal or not, had to be capable of receiving the sovereign. The lord or bishop would have vacated his apartment in deference to his superior. Haakon was returning to Bergen following the battle of Largs, where much of his fleet had been lost. The skill of the writer of *Haakon Haakonson's Saga* allows the imagination to people the now ruined, roofless shell:

'When he [Haakon] arrived at Kirkwall, he was confined to his bed by his disorder. Having lain for some nights, the illness abated and he was on foot for three days. On the first day he walked about his apartments; on the second he attended at the bishop's chapel to hear mass; and on the third he went to St Magnus's church, and walked round the shrine of St Magnus. He then ordered a bath to be prepared and got himself shaved. Some nights after, he relapsed and took again to his bed … On Sunday the royal corpse was carried into the upper hall and laid on a bier. The masters of the lights stood with tapers in their hands, and the whole hall was illuminated. All the people came to see the body.'

King Haakon's death effectively heralded the demise of Norway's direct hold over the *Nordreyjar*. Power now lay in the hands of earls who were no longer Norwegians but Scots. The Bishop's Palace gradually fell into disuse, although it did host another royal corpse in 1290, when that of seven-year-old Margaret, 'Maid of Norway', Haakon's great-granddaughter, was brought here from the ship taking her from Norway to Scone for her coronation as queen of Scots.

Then, just as the Reformation was about to bring down the curtain on Roman Catholicism and episcopacy, forward stepped Bishop Robert Reid (died 1558) to rescue the crumbling Bishop's Palace from oblivion. He stone-vaulted the ground floor, comprehensively

redesigned the hall, and erected a new round tower, Bishop Reid's Tower (*see left*), to house his private lodging. A nice finishing touch was the re-erection of an old stone statue – perhaps of Earl Rognvald, founder of the original cathedral and palace – in a niche on the outside wall of his new tower (*see right*). Why the bishop chose to build in so grand a manner is not clear, though the growing militarism of the Sinclairs may have played a part. As things turned out, within two years of Bishop Reid's death, Scotland was declared a Protestant country, and four years after that the Sinclairs too became history in Orkney. The new power in the islands was the thug Robert Stewart, Mary Queen of Scots' illegitimate half-brother. It was his son, Patrick, who built the impressive Earl's Palace beside the old bishop's residence.

EARL'S PALACE, KIRKWALL

Orkney

House of a tyrant

In the heart of Kirkwall, cheek-by-jowl with the Bishop's Palace, stands the Earl's Palace. By the time of Daniell's visit there was essentially just the one palace; episcopacy had long been abolished in Scotland, so there was no further function for a Bishop's Palace. Earl Patrick of Orkney, before that abolition but at a time when the see was vacant, had taken the opportunity to incorporate the ancient episcopal residence into his own grand new house in 1606. Earl Patrick has traditionally been seen as a tyrant, exercising control over his dominions with a cruelty that has become legendary. From the day 'Black Patie' took over his father's patrimony in 1592 to the day of his execution in Edinburgh 23 years later, he ruled the Northern Isles with an iron fist. So bereft was he of the era's basic standards of decency that his execution had to be delayed until he had learned to recite the Lord's Prayer. At his trial he was accused of 'extraordinary oppression and treasonable violence'. His tyranny manifested itself in numerous ways, including using forced labour to build his castles, as the trial transcript reveals:

'The said earl … has compelled the most part of the gentlemen tenants to work to him all manner of work and labour … in the stone quarry winning and bearing forth stones … loading his boats and shallops with stone and lime, and loosing [unloading] the same, building his park dykes, and all other sorts of servile and painful labour, without meat, drink or hire.'

Those Orcadians and Shetlanders compelled to do their master's bidding have long gone the way of all flesh, but the fruits of their forced labours survive. They include not only the spectacular Earl's Palace in Kirkwall but also a fine tower-house castle in the ancient capital of Shetland, Scalloway (*see right*).

The Earl's Palace is a building of extraordinary beauty and refinement. It is spacious and masterly planned, with an architectural enrichment that is delicate and scholarly. That such a building, without parallel elsewhere in Scotland, was built by the tyrant Earl Patrick makes it even more remarkable. But this was the age of the 'Renaissance Man' — individuals perfectly capable of displaying their cultured and refined tastes unimpeded by any twinge of conscience.

Earl Patrick's palace comprised an entirely new building of two ranges, linked to the redesigned Bishop's Palace to its west. The area in front, between the two palaces and the cathedral, was made into a spacious forecourt. The complex became known as the 'New Wark [work, i.e. building] of the Yards', indicating how the whole was drawn together into one great defensible enclosure castle. Time, though, has not been kindly to the Earl's Palace (*see left*), and since its abandonment as a noble house on the death there in 1688 of Bishop Murdoch, Orkney's last prelate, the grand courtyard has gone and so also the seamless link with the Bishop's Palace, rent asunder in the 19th century by the construction of a public road.

What remains, though, still has the power to impress: those two tall, large turrets on their chequered corbel bases at the corners of the tower wherein Earl Patrick had his private apartment; the two oriel windows (to the left of the elegant chimney stack), one circular and the other multi-angled, which bathed the great hall behind them in sunshine; and the elaborate entrance doorway (*see right*) over which Earl Patrick Stewart proudly displayed his own coat-of-arms and those of his king, James VI.

The feeling one gets on entering the front door is that this is no run-of-the-mill Scottish laird's house. The main stair, taking visitors up to the *piano nobile* (literally 'noble floor' – the level housing the main public rooms), makes that immediately apparent, for it is a handsome scale and platt (flight and landing), with broad landings linked by straight flights of steps. The impression made by climbing the staircase is further reinforced on entering the great hall at the top (*see right*). This must have been one of the noblest state rooms of any private castle in Scotland. Even in its present roofless condition it impresses – well proportioned, finely wrought and wonderfully lit by oriel windows to east and west and a great three-light window at the south end beside the stairs. The capacious main fireplace (one of two in the hall) is a massive 5m (15ft) wide, its flat-arched lintel carried on elaborate pilasters similar to those on the entrance doorway.

Another feeling one gets, though only after a good deal of inspection, is that the owner of this house was not just motivated by the needs of comfort and style but also by the requirement for privacy and security. Earl Patrick had his own suite of rooms beyond the top end of the great hall, well away from those occupied by his household officials and guests, which lay in the west range beyond the main stairs. And right beside the door into the great hall was the room of the steward, the man responsible for the smooth running of his master's house. One can visualize the earl's right-hand man peering out through the window overlooking the entrance court (*see left*), keeping a note of all those coming and going – both friend and foe.

CASTLE GIRNIGOE

Caithness, Highland
A tale of two towers

Two tall towers stand within 30m (100ft) of each other on a sliver of rock overlooking Sinclair's Bay. Far below, the powerful swell of the North Sea beats out its relentless rhythm. When Daniell visited, both towers had been abandoned to the birds for over a century (*see above*). Two centuries on, the elements have taken their toll on these impressive works of man, and the jagged pinnacle of the tower (*to the right in the photograph opposite*) — for some unaccountable reason known as Castle Sinclair – detached from the rest of the ruin, now looks like a rocket on its launch-pad.

The builders of Girnigoe were the Sinclair earls of Orkney and Caithness. In 1470, following James III's acquisition of the Northern Isles from the king of Norway, Earl William Sinclair exchanged his Orkney holdings for estates in Caithness, including Girnigoe. This led to the building of the huge Castle Girnigoe, straddling the narrow promontory between the North Sea and the narrow geo, or gully, behind. The 15th century was a boom time for tower-house builders (*another example is Cardoness, page 22*), and most conformed to a standard design. Girnigoe is basically like the others, with the lord's

hall half-way up, private chambers above and service offices below. But there are aberrations, such as the entrance passage at ground level and a sub-vault beneath, the attached kitchen block at one corner, and features unusual in tower houses, including an oriel window overlooking the rock-cut ditch to the west, and galleries projecting from the sides facing the water giving the family some fine views, weather permitting. Why two towers? The answer seems to lie in the decision by the 5th earl, in 1592, to resign his earldom to his son, reserving to himself a life rent.

Both noblemen had distinct households that needed to be separately housed (the situation is paralleled elsewhere, for example, at Huntingtower near Perth), leading at some point afterwards to the creation of a second residence. We know that the west tower, where the promontory joins the land, was built by 1607, for the date was noted as being carved on a window lintel by a visitor in 1701. The tower was originally four storeys high, though precious little survives today (*see above*). Which tower was occupied by whom will forever remain a mystery.

CASTLE OF OLD WICK

Caithness, Highland
A Viking legacy

In Caithness, slivers of rock thrusting out into the sea – and teetering towers built on them – seem to go together. As at Girnigoe (*page 108*), to the north of Wick, so also at Old Wick, to the south. But whereas there seems little doubt about the later medieval date of the former, the jury seems still to be out about the Castle of Old Wick, also known as the 'Old Man of Wick'. The problem at Old Wick is the lack of architectural clues in the tower's ruined shell (*see right*), coupled with the absence of archaeological excavation on the grass-covered spine of rock itself. The tower has four storeys, all unvaulted. The entrance was originally on the first floor. Other than the occasional window slit, and the ledges supporting the timber floors, the building is largely featureless. We can only assume that above the ground-floor cellar was the lord's hall, and àbove that his private apartment. This standard arrangement could lead one to think that the 'Old Man' isn't that old – perhaps constructed in the 14th century like the first generation of tower houses. But there are aspects that lead me to suspect that the 'Old Man' is considerably older. There were fireplaces, but they did not have flues rising up through the walls, but 'hingin' lums', smoke hoods attached to the inside faces. And there is no evidence for mural stairs or wall chambers either, just a poky latrine closet off the hall (recorded in the 19th century, before that part collapsed).

If we accept that the 'Old Man' is, say, 12th century, then it was built when Caithness and the Northern Isles were fully under the sway of the Norsemen, the descendants of the Vikings who settled there in the 9th century. So who might its lordly builder have been, and are there parallels elsewhere in the Norse dominions? The *Orkneyinga Saga*, written down about 1220, mentions four castles in the region: one on the island of Damsay, another on Wyre, the third in Kirkwall, and the fourth at Thurso (Caithness). It is the one on Wyre that is of the greatest interest today because the saga description is complemented by the physical remains themselves.

Cubbie Roo's Castle (*see left*) stands on a ridge overlooking Wyre Sound. Close by is the ruined 12th-century St Mary's Church, and the modern farm name, the Bu of Wyre, recalls the great Norse drinking hall that would have preceded the stone castle as the family residence. The saga tells us that about the year 1150 Kolbein Hruga, the young man who lived on the island, 'built a fine stone castle which was a strong defence'. Kubbie was a Norse nickname for Kolbein; hence the corruption of his name to Cubbie Roo. All that remains today of Kolbein Hruga's tower is its basement, 7m (23ft) square and with 2m- (6.5ft-) thick walls (almost identical to Old Wick). There is no ground-floor entrance, and the only features are two slit windows and a stone-lined water tank sunk into the floor. How high it stood is impossible to say, but three storeys would have given clear views south over the island of Gairsay to Kirkwall.

The building of castles by Norsemen such as Kolbein Hruga may seem surprising, for though they came from the same root as the Normans, by the 12th century their social and political culture was different from their southern kinsmen. But this is to ignore the remarkable degree of contact between the men from the north and the other castle-building societies. The *Orkneyinga Saga* itself recounts in fascinating detail Earl Rognvald of Orkney's three-year voyage on crusade to the Holy Land in the 1150s. The passage describing his successful attack on a Spanish castle includes missiles raining down on both camps, boiling pitch and brimstone being poured from the battlements, and the piles of burning faggots melting the lime holding the castle walls together. Such encounters must have made an impression on the Norsemen. In the unsettled, blood-spattered society of the Northern Isles there was surely a place for the castle.

The Norsemen's encounters with castles were not always hostile; once they had settled, there was peaceful contact with other nations, including Scotland. This included marriage alliances. Harald Maddadson, earl of Orkney and Caithness from 1139 to 1206, had an Orcadian mother and a Scottish father. And when Harald himself married, he took as his lady Affrica, daughter of the Earl Duncan of Fife, the builder of Cupar Castle. If any individual can now be credited with building the 'Old Man of Wick' then it surely must be Harald, ruler of Caithness for over 50 years.

DUNROBIN CASTLE
Sutherland, Highland
Formidable castle to fairytale château

On a tree-clad hillside overlooking the North Sea, a brisk walk from the town of Golspie, stands the architectural confection called Dunrobin Castle; the place could easily pass for Sleeping Beauty's castle. Even in Daniell's day, before the Victorians transformed it into the fairytale château we see today, the ancient stronghold of the earls of Sutherland had become an 'eye-catcher', a creation of man's to rival nature's brooding Beinn a'Bhragaidh mountain behind (*see above*). But even this great pile wasn't enough to satisfy George Granville Sutherland-Leveson-Gower, 2nd marquis of Stafford, 20th earl and 2nd duke of Sutherland, and one of the richest men in Great

Britain, who inherited Dunrobin in 1841. With eight children and their spouses to think of, he financed the building of the vast mansion we now admire (*see right*) 'for the very numerous members of the family, to induce their prolonged stay together in the north' (their chief residence was Trentham Park, Staffordshire).

Almost everything we see today from the sprawling grounds around Dunrobin dates from the 1840s, when the castle and gardens were redesigned by Sir Charles Barry, who had just designed the new Houses of Parliament at Westminster.

Remarkably, given the magnitude of the 2nd duke's building work, there lie at Dunrobin's core parts of the medieval castle built by his ancestors. The most conspicuous early survivals belong to 1641–44, including the crow-stepped, turreted ranges along the north and west sides of the inner court, their pedimented windows emblazoned with the arms and intitials IES and ACS for John, the 14th earl, and Anne, his second countess. But it is the building closing off the east side of that inner court that intrigues me most,

a tall stone tower (*see right*) that stands out proudly on the right in Daniell's closer view (*see above*). By then, that tower had been altered considerably. Each of the four floors inside had been vaulted over in stone, and externally the wall head had been rebattlemented with turrets at each corner. But take away those vaults and that battlemented parapet, and we might just be looking at the tower built by the 1st earl of Sutherland in the early 13th century, or even his Norse predecessor in the 12th. The parallels with the Castle of

Old Wick (*page 110*), 68km (42 miles) away up the coast, are striking. Both share a similar footprint – Dunrobin 8 x 7m (26 x 23ft) to Old Wick's 9 x 7m (29 x 23ft) – have no stairs, and are entered at first-floor level. The iron yett (cross-barred gate) now hanging on a nearby wall may be from Dunrobin's original doorway. If indeed the tower is as old as this, then Dunrobin can claim to being the oldest continuously inhabited house in Scotland, older even than Dunvegan (*see page 92*).

DORNOCH CASTLE

Sutherland, Highland
A bishop's castle

On the north shore of the Dornoch Firth, in the lea of the sandy links, nestles the pretty town of Dornoch, ancient capital of Sutherland. The place rose to prominence in the early 13th century when Bishop Gilbert relocated his cathedral from Halkirk, in the far north of his Caithness diocese, to its most southerly border. Bishop Gilbert was a Scot, not a Norwegian, and he probably felt that the greater distance he could put between his *cathedra* (bishop's seat) and Norse-held Orkney the better. His new cathedral was ready for worship in 1239, and so, we may assume, was his new episcopal residence just across the road to its south.

What became of that first residence is unknown. By the time of Daniell's visit, Dornoch Castle consisted of a quadrangular palace centred on a courtyard and dominated at one corner by an imposing five-storey tower house (*see above*). The latter, still standing and now a comfortable hotel (*see right*), was built around 1500 but subsequently underwent much change – prompted not just by the Reformation of 1560 but also by the fire that swept through the building in 1570. The hand of nearby Dunrobin's marquis and countess of Stafford (*page 114*) in its refurbishment is evident from the panel carved with their arms and dated 1814.

Medieval bishops had to live somewhere, and as they were invariably scions of aristocratic families their residences took the form of castles, or at least fortified palaces. Bishop Gilbert of Caithness was no exception. Born into the mighty house of Moray (de Moravia), he was probably brought up at Duffus Castle, near Elgin, one of the finest surviving motte-and-bailey castles in Scotland. Before becoming bishop in 1222, Gilbert served as archdeacon of the diocese of Moray, and would have visited Bishop Brice's fine episcopal residence at Spynie, near Elgin, then the site of the cathedral. Spynie Palace still stands, albeit in ruin. The ruins visitors see today (*see left, as pictured by Thomas Grose c. 1789*) date from the 14th century, and share with Dornoch the quadrangular courtyard, dominated at one corner by a vast tower house, the largest by volume in Scotland. Spynie can also claim to be the most complete medieval bishop's residence surviving in Scotland, rivalled only by the awesome castle of the archbishops of Scotland at St Andrews (*page 142*).

Bishops and archbishops weren't just 'soldiers of Christ', they were often real soldiers, fighting the good fight alongside their fellow countrymen. Bishop Wishart of Glasgow (died 1316), whose fine stone effigy can still be seen in the crypt of his cathedral, offered Robert the Bruce far more than just spiritual leadership during the bitter Wars of Independence with England. And two prelates – Archbishop Alexander of St Andrews and Bishop George of the Isles – were among the 5000 Scots who fell at the battle of Flodden in 1513. Bishop Gilbert of Caithness fought English domination in the spiritual sphere, resisting attempts by the archbishop of York to control the Scottish church. Unlike two former bishops of Caithness, who died grisly deaths, Gilbert was fortunate to pass peacefully away in his bed at Dornoch Castle in 1245. His body was laid to rest in his cathedral church next door. Sadly, his effigy does not survive, only Alexander Carrick's chunky-lettered tablet of 1924 (*see right*).

KINNAIRD HEAD CASTLE

Aberdeenshire
New wine in an old bottle

Kinnaird Head (*cinn na h'airde* in Gaelic) means 'at the head of the point of land'. One look at a map is enough to show that this particular point of land beside Fraserburgh is no ordinary promontory. It lies on Scotland's north-east shoulder at the place where the coastline turns through 90 degrees. Quite why the Frasers of Philorth (the ancient name of the parish) chose to build a castle on this exposed headland in the mid-16th century is uncertain. Daniell illustrates all too well the drama of its location, buffeted by the raging North Sea storms (*see above*); not the place one would normally choose to live.

Perhaps the Frasers never saw it as a family residence – their main seat was inland from Kinnaird Head – but as a focal point in their grand scheme to develop the village of Faithlie into a thriving port. They succeeded, and Faithlie grew into the burgh of Fraserburgh.

The Frasers would have seen the opportunities presented by Scotland's growing trade with continental Europe. They would also have seen how pivotal Kinnaird Head was to crews attempting to navigate around the north-east coast, and their tower house may have served from the outset as a beacon for shipping. Two centuries later, in 1786, the newly created Northern Lighthouse Board recognized that same importance and chose the old tower as the location for one of the first four lighthouses designed to cover Scotland's long and complex coastline. (The others were at North Ronaldsay in Orkney, Eilean Glas on Lewis, and the Mull of Kintyre in Argyll.) Kinnaird Head was the first to be lit, in 1787. Both the tower and the lighthouse it supports stand yet (*see right*), the most unlikely bedfellows; the proverbial 'new wine in an old bottle'.

The combination of old tower and new lighthouse is unparalleled. It is also lucky to have survived. Had Robert Stevenson, the great lighthouse engineer and builder of the Bell Rock lighthouse, had his way, the tower would have been demolished in 1824 and replaced by a purpose-built structure. That the grandfather of Robert Louis Stevenson was dissuaded from this act of folly is probably down to another of Scotland's literary giants, Sir Walter Scott, who accompanied Stevenson on an expedition around Scotland on the Board's *Pharos* in 1814. Scott's antiquarian sentiments appear to have restricted Stevenson to demolishing the structures around the tower only – all except the enigmatically named 'Wine Tower'. These structures are all shown by Daniell. What Daniell couldn't illustrate, of course, was the damage wrought by the Board to the old tower's interior. Other than the vaulted ground storey, which was retained, floors were ripped out, new doors and windows added, and the entire top storey removed and replaced by a lantern. The old stairs were replaced by Robert Stevenson's fine spiral stair (*right*).

Not only was Kinnaird Head the Board's first operational lighthouse; it subsequently earned a further accolade as the site of the Board's first permanent radio beacon, for use in fog. The lighthouse no longer functions as a focal point for navigation, for it was decommissioned in 1991 and replaced by a small automated light nearby. Instead, the castle tower now serves as the focus of the Scottish Lighthouse Museum – appropriately, since Fraserburgh was where it all began more than two hundred years ago.

DUNNOTTAR CASTLE

Aberdeenshire
Safe house

Dunnottar must be one of the most spectacularly sited ancient strongholds in Scotland – a lonely rock plateau thrusting out from the precipitous Kincardineshire coast into the chilly depths of the North Sea, and approachable only over a narrow, treacherous tongue of land. Its origins as a safe house reach back into the mists of time. By the time Guillaume le Clerc featured it in his epic tale *Roman de Fergus* around 1200, it had clearly acquired a reputation as a magical place, the home of a scythe-wielding hag, protector of the Shining Shield, the winning of which would be Fergus's supreme test in his quest for the beautiful maiden he pined for. By around 1400, Dunnottar had become the home of the

real-life Sir William Keith, grand marischal (marshal) of Scotland. In this post, he was responsible for the sovereign's stables and travel arrangements. He probably built the great tower house that dominates the view from the land (*see above*). When, in 1458, his grandson was given an earldom by a grateful James II, he took the title 'earl marischal'. Nicholas Guendeville's early 18th-century depiction of the 'riding and downsitting of the Parliament' (*see right*) shows the grand marischal both in his place in the procession (alongside the grand commissioner and grand constable) and at his post in Parliament, to the right of the table holding the crown, sceptre and sword of state – the Honours of Scotland.

CARTE POUR DONNER UNE IDÉE GENERALE DU GOUVERNEMENT D'ECOSSE; L'ORDRE DE LA MARCHE OU CAVALCADE DE L'ASSEMBLÉE DE SON PARLEMENT; ET CELUI DE LA SÉANCE DE CET ILUSTRE CORPS.

Remarque Generale

L'Ecosse se gouverne à peu près par les mêmes loix que l'Angleterre, qui consistent au Droit Civil, aux Ordonnances des Rois, et aux Actes du Parlement, qu'on appelle Loix Municipalles. L'Autorité Royale sur l'Ecosse à les mêmes prérogatives qu'en Angleterre, pour ajourner, proroger ou dissoudre le Parlement, augmenter ou diminuer le nombre des Deputez qui le composent. Il est laitre de la Iustice et des Loix. Le pouvoir de faire la guerre ou la paix est uniquement entre ses mains; tous les Officiers de Mer et de terre dependent de luy, et toutes les forces du Royaume. Il peut eriger des Foires, mettre des imposts sur les droits sur toute sorte de Marchandise, qui entrent ou qui sortent de ce Royaume. Il peut encore obliger ses Sujets à luy fournir 2000 hommes de pied et 2000 de Cavallerie. Le Parlement que l'on represente icy est composé de 4 ordres, savoir: La Haute Noblesse, le Clergé, les Deputez des Provinces, et ceux des Villes et des Bourgs. Le Clergé est representé par les Archevesques et ceux de St André de Glascow, et par les Evesques du Royaume. L'Archevesque de St André est Primat du Royaume; les Evesques sont Pairs du Royaume et comme ceux d'Angleterre des Cours particulieres où ils jugent sans Colleques, et tous les Actes s'expedient en leur nom, et non en celui du Roi. Ils president aux Sinodes Provinciaux de leurs Provinces qui se tiennent deux fois l'an, en Avril et en Octobre pour la reformation des mœurs. La Noblesse est divisée en deux Classes. Ceux du Premier ordre, sont les Seigneurs ou les Pairs du Royaume, qui sont les Ducs, les Marquis, les Comtes, les Vicomtes et les Barons; le nombre en est presque aussi grand qu'en Angleterre. La Seconde Noblesse comprend les Petis Barons qui sont les Nobles que les Provinces deputent pour assister en leur nom au Parlement. Ils avoient autrefois le droit d'y Comparoitre, ou d'y envoyer tel nombre de Deputez qu'ils vouloient, mais la grande depense qu'ils etoient obligez de faire les porta à suplier Iacques I. de les en dispenser qu'il leur fut accordé par un Acte de 1430, par lequel le Roy leur laissoit la liberté d'y venir en personne ou d'y envoyer des Deputez sans enfreindre le nombre. Ils perdirent ce Privilege par leur negligence ou par le malheur des Guerres civiles, de sorte que pour rétablir l'ancienne forme du Gouvernement, Iacques VI ordonna que chaque Province choisiroit deux Nobles à la pluralité des Voix, et que les Deputez qu'elles auroient Eleus auroient le rang et la qualité de Petis Barons, et seroient appelez Commissaires des Comtez. Le peuple se represente dans le Parlement par les Deputez des Villes et des Bourgs. Lors qu'il plaist au Roi de convoquer

Suite de la Remarque.

son Parlement; Les Deputez s'etant rendus à Edimbourg capitale de l'Ecosse, ils s'assemblent à l'Abbaye de Ste Croix, ou Holyroode houle, pour proceder à la marche, ou Cavalcade, telle qu'on la represente ici; s'etant rendus au Parlement en cette ceremonie, le Grand Commissaire se place sur son Throne, et près de lui les Grands Officiers de la Couronne, et aux deux côtés: les Prelats et les Pairs seculiers; Les Deputez des Provinces à la droite et ceux des Bourgs à la gauche. Les Ornemens Royaux sont mis sur une table par le Grand Connétable et par le Grand Maréchal. Après la priere faite par l'Evesque d'Edimbourg, on fait la Lecture de la Liste des Deputez: en suite le Grand Chancelier s'approchant du Throne se met à Genoux et reçoit des mains du Grand Commissaire, la Commission du Roi, qu'il donne à un Secretaire pour en faire la lecture. On lit en suite la Formule qui est la maniere et l'ordre de l'Assemblée, après quoi Lion Roi d'Armes descent du Throne et place les Seigneurs et Deputez selon leurs rangs. Le Grand Commissaire declare en suite les intentions du Roi qui sont plus amplement expliquées par le grand Chancelier; on fait prêter serment aux Deputez et on nomme des Commissaires pour dresser la reponse à la lettre du Roi. On procede en suite à l'Election des Commissaires, appelés Seigneurs ou Lords, des Articles qui doivent être proposez au Parlement: pour cela on choisit 8 Evesques, 8 Milords, 8 Chevaliers et 8 Bourgeois qui sont les 4 ordres du Royaume. Voicy la maniere de proceder à cette Election: Les Evesques choisissent les Seigneurs qui sont à Duc, 2 Marquis et 6 Comtes. Les Seigneurs nomment les Ecclesiastiques qui sont ordinairement les 2 Archevesques avec 6 Evesques. Ces 16 Commissaires avec les Grands Officiers de la Couronne, qui sont toûjours dans toutes les affaires choisissent les 18 autres, savoir 8 pour les Provinces et 8 pour les Bourgs. Tous ces préliminaires étant achevés, on reconduit le Grand Commissaire dans le même ordre: en revient les autres jours au Parlement sans ceremonie. Il y a encore un Parlement fixe à Edimbourg qui fut etabli par Iacques V. avant celui-ci; il y en avoit un mouvant qui alloit par les Villes rendre Iustice et interpreter les Loix. Les Ecossais ont encore quelques Cours souveraines de Grands Iusticiers pour les matieres criminelles de chaque Province. Outre ces Officiers Ordinaires, il y a encore un Vicomte hereditaire qui juge les causes civiles et criminelles.

Le Throne du Roy	1	Le Grand Maréchal	7	Les Archevesques	14	Palais representant l'Ecosse,
Le Grand Commissaire	2	Milord Grefier	8	Les Comtes	15	tenant d'une main une Epée,
Le Grand Chancelier	3	Secretaire d'Etat	9	Les Evesques et Vicomtes	16	de l'autre les Armes d'Ecosse
Grands Officiers de la Couronne	4	Lion Roi d'Armes	10	Les Barons	17	foulant des Trophées à ses pieds
Table pour la Couronne et	5	Le Grand Huissier	11	Les Deputez et Commissaires des Comtes et des Bourgs	18	elle a sur son sein le Chardon
L'Epée du Roy	5	Herauts et Pourfuyants	12			
Le Grand Connétable	6	Les Raporteurs des Voix	13			Chapeau de la Liberté	19

L'ORDRE DE LA MARCHE DES DEPUTÉZ DU PARLEMENT D'ECOSSE, LORS QU'ILS VONT ET REVIENENT LE PREMIER IOUR DE LEUR ASSEMBLÉE AU PARLEMENT.

Porte du Parlement

Trompettes

Pourfuivans

Les Commissaires des Comtes, et des Bourgs, et des Villes

Lords Advocats

Lords Barons

Les Evesques

Les Archevesques

Comtes et Vicomtes

L'Abbaye de Sainte Croix, ou Holyroode houle

Les Gardes du Roy

Les Comtes

Les Vicomtes

Herauts d'...

Trompettes du Roy

Pourfuivans

Gr. Marechal

Gr. Ecuyer

Capitaine des Gardes du Roy

Le Grand Commissaire

Gr. Connetable

Lyon Roy d'Armes

Le Grand Huissier

Marq. qui porte la couronne du Roy

Massier

Massier

Massier

Celui qui porte la ... du Roy.

Cm. porte le Sceptre du Roy.

Cm. Porte l'Epée du Roy

Les Commissaires des Comtes, Bourgs, et Villes

Avec Privilege de Nosseigneurs les Etats de Holl: et de Westfrise.

Freindis (social equals) Kin (blood relations) Lord Lady Tenentis (tenants)

Constable Marshal Chaplain Steward

Gunners Door Wards Blacksmiths Carters Clerk of the Writing Office Clerk of the Chapel Cook Bard Piper Doctor Gentlemen Servants Ladies-in-Waiting

Men-at-Arms Farriers Messengers Muleteers Assistant Clerks Sacristan Musicians Stonemasons Carpenters Wardrobers Tailor Laundress

Armourers Porters Boatmen Stable Lads Choir Boys Undercooks Larderers Bakers Alewife Poulterers Gardeners

To appreciate how a medieval castle such as the earl marischal's at Dunnottar functioned, we have to know something of the composition of a great nobleman's household. Because the castle had to function variously as family home, soldiers' barracks, guest house, estate office, law court and prison, the household was both large and varied. At the head were a handful of key officials. The hierarchy of the lord's household is shown in the diagram (*see left*). They included the marshal, the position the Keiths held in the royal household; the steward, to whom fell the task of ensuring the smooth running of the place; the constable, responsible for security; and the chaplain, who acted as his lord's secretary, but also managed the spiritual side of things. Each official had charge of a host of assistants, lower-ranking servants and menials. Under the constable were the porters, who guarded the castle gates, and the door wards or ushers, who watched the doors leading into the lord's presence. Under the chaplain were the clerk of the writing office and the clerk of the chapel, the latter in turn supervising others, including the sacristan and choirboys. In the kitchens were cooks, bakers, poulterers – and the ale-wife (for some reason ale was always brewed by a woman).

Elsewhere were the tailor, laundress, wardrobers and gardeners, and the minstrels in their gallery (*such as those seen right, from the painted ceiling at Crathes Castle, Aberdeenshire*). In the stables, under the marshal's watchful eye, were the farriers, carters and messengers who went hither and yon about the realm with dispatches. Attending directly on their lord and lady were gentleman servants and ladies-in-waiting, including (if they were Highlanders) a bard, and if a Lowlander a 'fool' or jester. The wooden portrait of James V's fool (*see above*) once adorned the royal presence chamber in Stirling Castle – one of the famous 'Stirling Heads'.

Of course, not every baronial household would have been so extensive; everything was relative. But somebody of the rank and station of the earl marischal might well have commanded something approaching the complement given above, numbering in excess of 100 people, most of them male.

Of the many remarkable events in Dunnottar's long history, one in particular stands out – the hiding away there of the Honours of Scotland in the winter of 1651–52. When the Scots proclaimed Charles II as their king in 1649, shortly after his father's beheading, Oliver Cromwell was furious. And when in June 1650 Charles arrived in Scotland for his coronation, the commander of the New Model Army was compelled to invade. By the time Cromwell captured Edinburgh Castle, however, he found that the Honours had already been spirited north to Scone for the coronation ceremony. He followed in hot pursuit. The Scots, unable to return the Honours to Edinburgh following the coronation, instead removed them to 'the hous of Dunnottor, thair to be keepit by the Earle Marischal till farther ordouris'.

The story of how George Ogilvie of Barras, governor of Dunnottar, and his men withstood the siege of Cromwell's army for eight bitter winter months; of how the Honours of Scotland were smuggled out under the very noses of the English and hidden in nearby Kinneff Kirk; and of how they lay there for eight long years, is one of the most well-kent tales of Scottish history. One account of the smuggling has them lowered over the castle walls to a woman pretending to gather seaweed on the beach far below. The more popular, but far less plausible, account has Mrs Granger, the local minister's wife, and her serving woman as the heroines of the piece. Having got permission from the English commander to go into the castle on the pretext of visiting the governor's wife, they emerged, Mrs Granger with the crown and sceptre under her skirts,

and her serving woman the far longer sword of state in a bundle of flax! The story goes that the breaks in the sword blade and scabbard resulted from the attempt to make the concealment more effective. When the English eventually stormed the castle, they found the safe empty. The memorial tablet in Kinneff Kirk to the Reverend Granger and his good lady has the Honours emblazoned upon it (*see left*).

One item of regalia wasn't smuggled out to Kinneff but cunningly retained by George Ogilvie as a memento – the elaborate sword belt (*see above*). In 1790 it was rediscovered by chance, built into a garden wall at his house of Barras, and only returned to its rightful place in the Crown Room in Edinburgh Castle in 1892.

BROUGHTY CASTLE

City of Dundee
Defence of the realm

Broughty Castle guards the entrance to the Firth of Tay. Daniell painted it from the east, looking up the estuary towards Dundee and Dundee Law (*see above*). The estuary is barely 1km wide at this point. 'Broughty' is derived from *broch*, meaning a strong point, plus the name of the river. Quite when 'the strong point on the Tay' became a strongpoint is not known; in medieval times, the sea-girt rock was called Partencraig, 'crab rock', suggesting more of an affinity with fishing than with fighting. We do know that the present

castle (*pictured right*) was built around 1490, shortly after the second Lord Gray received a royal charter to the 'rock of Bruchty', and with it a licence to build 'a castle and fortress, with ramparts, iron bars, marchicoulis [wall-head defences], drawbridges and other necessary defences'.

The decision to fortify may well have been prompted by an increased English naval threat. Only the previous year (1489), five heavily

armed English vessels had been intercepted off the Fife coast and captured. And no sooner had the royal seal been affixed to Lord Gray's charter than three more English ships were forced onto sandbanks near Broughty. James IV's realm was in peril, and the need for strong defences 'at the entrance of two of our Soverane's maist special rivers' was paramount. On the Tay Broughty was seen as the key. The date 1496 used to be visible high up near the tower house's battlements, indicating that Lord Gray had fulfilled his obligation within six years. The rush to build Broughty Castle seems not to have been justified by events, for there is no record that the place saw any action during the rest of James IV's reign. Indeed, Broughty seems only to have figured in two national emergencies in its entire 450-year history. Neither episode flattered Broughty's credentials as a 'defence of the realm'.

Broughty's first participation in a national emergency was an embarrassment. In September 1547, the duke of Somerset led an English army across the border in an attempt to intimidate Scotland into allowing a marriage between Edward VI of England and Mary Queen of Scots – the so-called 'Rough Wooing' – and at the Battle of Pinkie (near Musselburgh) on 10 September he inflicted terrible casualties on the earl of Arran's army. The Scottish military authorities, attempting to regroup after the débâcle, must have wished Lord Gray had never built Broughty in the first place, for within a fortnight of the battle Broughty was doing sterling service – as an English garrison fort.

To be fair to Lord Gray's architect, it wasn't so much the weakness of the place that proved its undoing – though its new English commander, Sir Andrew Dudley, did describe it as 'liker a keeper's lodge than a fort'. Its capture had more to do with the confused loyalties of Lord Gray himself, who much preferred that Mary should marry a Protestant Englishman rather than a Catholic Frenchman. For the next two and a half years, the English garrison not only held out at Broughty, but made life difficult for folk living around the Firth. They proved to be the proverbial 'thorn in the flesh', occupying Dundee and threatening Perth and St Andrews, pillaging in Angus and Fife, on one occasion kidnapping 'all the nuns and many gentlemen's daughters' in Elcho Nunnery, shooting at vessels attempting to enter and leave the Tay, and even firing at 'horsemen that pricketh amongst the hills'. All the Scots could do was bemoan the fact that *'our auld ynemies of England, being in the hous of Bruchtie, ar apperandly to invaid the haill cuntre, and to burn, herey* [harry]*, slay and destroy'.*

But when in 1548 the Scots finally agreed to their queen marrying the French dauphin, the garrison's fate was sealed. The arrival in Scotland of a massive French force shortly thereafter eventually forced the English out of their main 'bolt hole' at Haddington (East Lothian). The victors next turned their attention to Broughty, and in February 1550, the garrison surrendered and were allowed to go free. Broughty's first participation in the defence of the realm had ended; unfortunately, it had spent the entire war on the wrong side.

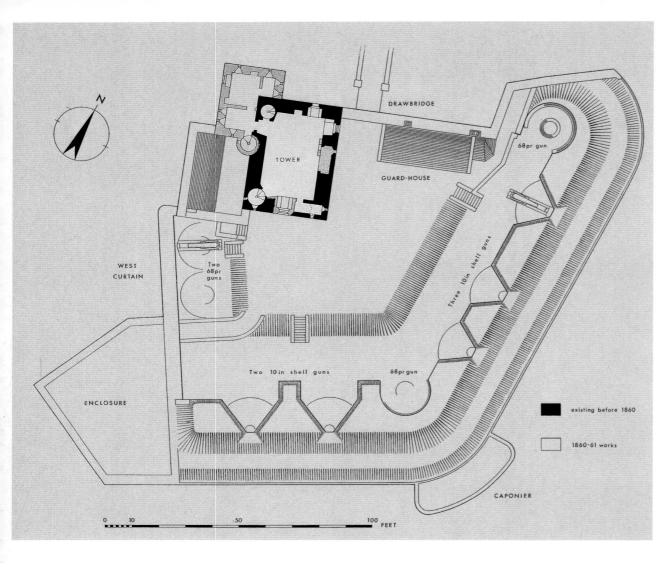

N

DRAWBRIDGE

TOWER

GUARD-HOUSE

68 pr gun

WEST
CURTAIN

Two
68 pr
guns

Three 10 in shell guns

ENCLOSURE

Two 10 in shell guns

68 pr gun

■ existing before 1860

□ 1860-61 works

CAPONIER

0   10   50   100 FEET

Broughty's second and last participation in the defence of the realm came three hundred years later, in the later 19th century. It was nowhere near as embarrassing, or as threatening, as the first, but even so it hardly covered the military authorities in glory. The threat came not from the English this time, but from the Russians, the French and the Germans – in that order. The military were slow getting their act together. Although they had identified the potential of Broughty's 'mouldering tower' to become a coastal defence battery to counter the Russian naval threat in the 1850s, the Crimean War came and went without anything being done. It took Lord

Tennyson's poem – 'Storm! Storm! Riflemen form! Ready be against the Storm!' – published in the *Times* of 9 May 1859 in response to a French invasion threat, to persuade them actually to do something. Early in 1860, work began on converting the medieval castle into 'a solid piece of modern masonry bristling all over with guns'. The designer, Robert Rowand Anderson, a 26-year-old working in the Royal Engineers' office in Edinburgh Castle, went on to become arguably Scotland's leading Victorian architect, creating such masterpieces as the National Portrait Gallery in Edinburgh; Broughty was his first commission. (*A plan of Broughty is shown above*).

Lieut. Coyle R.E. Lieut. Boase Major Fergusson Capth. Fergusson.

To accommodate the sergeant and 14 men, Anderson had the old tower house gutted and a second tower attached to its landward side. To house the guns, he removed much of the old curtain wall and towers (*Daniell depicts a fine round tower, which was still standing at the time of his visit, see page 134*), and built a massive earthen angled battery facing out to sea and across the Firth to Fife. And there sat the four mighty 68-pounders with a range of 2000m (2250yds) and five 10-inch guns with a range of 1500m (1700yds), primed and ready to take on the French. But they never showed, and the only shots fired were a 42-gun salute to mark Prince Albert's death in December 1861.

Perhaps it was just as well that Sir Rowand Anderson forsook military design for a career in mainstream architecture, given what was said about Broughty by a Captain Grant in 1888:

'badly built, badly designed, and utterly useless for the purpose… A fort such as this could never defend our river, for its total demolition would only afford an enemy an hour's pleasant and agreeable recreation, unharassed by any thoughts of possible danger to themselves.'

Damning words, which condemned much of Anderson's work. What we see today (*pictured on page 139*) is largely the result of rearming measures done as the century drew to its close.

The men from the Tay Division Royal Engineers (Volunteers), raised in 1888, manned the new armament (*see above*). Works were still being carried out at the castle right up to 1942, when the defence post was built on top of the tower house (*see left*). There is no record that any of them was ever put to the test.

ST ANDREWS CASTLE

Fife
Church and state

The city of St Andrews was the headquarters of the Scottish church in the middle ages. Its great cathedral, whose imposing remains dominate Daniell's view (*see above*), was the largest in the land, and its associated castle (on the far right of the painting) among the strongest of fortresses. As the principal residence of Scotland's leading clergyman, the castle was the setting for many important events. Robert the Bruce stayed there in March 1309 while presiding over his first Parliament. James I received his education there from Bishop Wardlaw, founder of Scotland's first university in 1410. So too did his son, the warlike James II, who was given practical advice from Bishop Kennedy as to how to deal with over-mighty nobles like the Black Douglases; Kennedy demonstrated that a full sheaf of arrows was impossible to break, but that each arrow taken singly presented no such problem. James took the lesson to heart.

Today, little remains of the stone castle built by Bishop Roger around 1200, for that was extensively damaged during the bloody Wars of Independence in the 14th century. The present complex dates from the late 14th century (*photograph shows the castle from the top of St Rule's tower with the cathedral's east gable in the foreground*).

Bishop Trail (1385–1401) masterminded the rebuilding (*the seal shown to the left is his*). But even this residence was subsequently greatly altered, mostly during the first half of the 16th century, at a time of growing national crisis and heightened tension between church and state.

The death of Archbishop Alexander, illegitimate son of King James IV, on the battlefield of Flodden in 1513 began the crisis. His untimely death led to an unseemly scramble for the vacant see. The eventual victor, Archbishop Forman, was swiftly succeeded by Archbishop James Beaton, and it was he who set about transforming Bishop Trail's castle into a formidable artillery fortress, replete with towers bristling with guns. Beaton clearly anticipated trouble.

By the time it arrived, James Beaton had been succeeded (1538) by his nephew David Beaton (*see left*), bishop of Mirepoix (France), commendator of Arbroath Abbey (Angus), and shortly afterwards became a cardinal. He vehemently rejected the rising tide of Protestantism, and was unyielding in his opposition to the proposed marriage of Mary Queen of Scots to the son of Henry VIII of England. His arrival centre-stage set Scotland on an irreversible course towards conflict.

The crunch came in March 1546 when Beaton had the Protestant preacher George Wishart burned at the stake, right in front of his castle so he could get a grandstand view. The grisly act succeeded only in making him more enemies, and in May a band of Protestant lairds contrived to get into his fortress disguised as stonemasons. They seized and murdered the cardinal, then dangled his naked corpse from the battlements wrapped only in a pair of sheets.

The cardinal's murder was the opening scene in the drama of the Scottish Reformation. Almost immediately, the earl of Arran, in his capacity as regent, besieged the castle. It would be one of the most bitterly contested sieges in Scotland's history, dragging on for 14 months and involving that other 'giant' of the Scottish Reformation, John Knox (*see right*), the fiery Protestant preacher and formerly Wishart's 'minder'. It has left behind one of the most remarkable examples of siege engineering to survive anywhere in Europe: the mine and countermine.

Six months into the siege, the French ambassador in London reported that Arran's men were digging a mine beneath the castle walls in an attempt to force an entry. The defenders, he noted, were doing their utmost to forestall them by counter-mining. The fruits of their combined labours, filled in immediately after the siege ended, were rediscovered in 1879 and are now accessible for all to see.

The mine (*see left*) was a spacious, stepped corridor, high and wide enough for pack animals to be used in it to remove the rock more speedily. Surprisingly, the entrance to the mine was situated within 40m (130ft) of the castle walls, demonstrating just how closely fought medieval siege warfare was, even at this late date and well into the era of gunpowder artillery.

The countermine (*see right*), by contrast, was a cramped affair, testifying to the desperation of the defenders, who by now included John Knox. In fact, they made two false starts in their fevered attempt to locate the mine before they succeeded in breaking through. Eventually, the stalemate was broken only when a heavily armed French force arrived and opened up a murderous artillery bombardment. The castle walls were ripped apart. An eyewitness described the devastation:

'Thate daye thai schote downe all the battellyne and caiphouse of the seytowre: and all this daye tha schote upone the easte parte of the castell … at the hall and chapell, and dislodged us of that parte be downputting of the riffis and sklatis'.

EDINBURGH CASTLE

City of Edinburgh
Principal strength of the realm

Mighty Edinburgh Castle has dominated its surroundings majestically for centuries. For 3000 years tribal chiefs and sovereign kings have held sway from the castle rock. In ancient times they called it Din Eidyn, 'the stronghold of Eidyn', though who or what Eidyn was is a mystery (legend tells of a local giant called the Red Etin). By the 6th century AD, the rock was the fortress of Mynyddog 'the Magnificent', king of the Gododdin, the native British tribe. Then came the marauding Angles, around 638, and ever since then the rock has been known by its English name – Edinburgh.

In the middle ages, Edinburgh became Scotland's chief royal castle. It was also the main arsenal of the realm, housing such monsters as Mons Meg (*see right*), one of the most remarkable of all medieval guns. It was, too, the nation's safety deposit box, holding the crown jewels and the state archives. By the time of King James VI's birth there in June 1566, the castle was 'the first and principall strengthe of the realme'. When James left for London in 1603 to become King James I of England also, the castle became little more than a garrison fortress.

Edinburgh's origins as a royal castle reach back to David I's reign in the 12th century. The youngest of King Malcolm III and Queen Margaret's six sons, David became effective ruler of southern Scotland as early as 1113. This 'most vigorous and courteous of kings' began the process of settling an immigrant aristocracy, the Normans, on Scottish soil, a development that continued after his death in 1153, under the encouragement of his two grandsons who succeeded him, Malcolm IV 'the Maiden' (*depicted to his grandfather's right on the decorated initial from a charter granted to Kelso Abbey in 1159, see left*) and William I 'the Lion' (died 1214).

David was born in Dunfermline about 1080, but had been brought up at the court of Henry I of England, William the Conqueror's son; Henry had married David's elder sister, Matilda. While in England, David observed at first hand Anglo-Norman ways and customs, and when he returned to the land of his birth, he brought with him an Anglo-Norman education, an Anglo-Norman wife, and a large following of Anglo-Norman knights. Life in Scotland was never going to be quite the same again.

His legacy was immense. He reorganized the church and introduced the new monastic orders, including the Augustinians to nearby Holyrood Abbey; he established towns such as Edinburgh and Canongate; he built mints for the striking of coin; and he forced the pace on the 'feudalizing' of Scotland. One thing is for sure – it was boom time for the building industry, and alongside the new cathedrals, monasteries, parish churches and towns arose the castles, the most potent symbol of the new order in Scotland.

They included Edinburgh atop its rock. Nothing now remains of King David's royal stronghold other than the little chapel named in honour of David's saintly mother, where he and Queen Maud heard mass each morning. St Margaret's Chapel stands on the highest part of the rock, and its delightful interior has a fine chevroned chancel arch (*right*). It is the oldest building in the castle, indeed in all Edinburgh.

Edinburgh Castle has an air of awesome impregnability about it, sufficient to have moved the poet John Taylor in 1618 to wax lyrical about it being 'so strongly grounded, bounded and founded that by force of man it can never be confounded'. Yet it was confounded, time and again. Edward I of England, 'Hammer of the Scots', battered the fortress into submission over three days in 1296, during those heady first days of the Wars of Independence. And a feat of derring-do by King Robert the Bruce's nephew, Sir Thomas Randolph, retook it in March 1314, shortly before Bruce's great victory over Edward II at Bannockburn. Randolph's men inched their way up the precipitous north face, overlooking what is now Princes Street Gardens, and caught the English garrison off-guard. And so it went, back and forth throughout the Wars of Independence.

One siege was so protracted it became known as 'the Lang Siege', when Sir William Kirkcaldy of Grange's men, still loyal to Mary Queen of Scots (who had just abdicated) held out for 18 months between 1571 and 1573 against James Douglas, earl of Morton, regent for the infant James VI. An English spy, sent north to assess the castle's strength in support of Morton, reported back that 'no mining can prevail in this rock but only battery with ordnance to beat down the walls'. And that's what they did, battering down the walls with heavy guns. Even then it took ten days of bombardment before the mighty David's Tower (named in honour of David II, Bruce's son) was brought crashing down. In its place Regent Morton built a great curved artillery defence, the Half-Moon Battery, unique in design and giving Edinburgh

Attempt to Surprise Edingb.^h Castle.

Castle an appearance unrivalled anywhere else in the world (*left*). The castle endured further sieges, including one in 1715 when James the Pretender, son of the late James VII and II, tried to wrest the throne back for the Stuarts; a contemporary cartoon (*see right*) depicts the Jacobites attempting to surprise the castle by storming the ancient postern on the west (back) side. When James's son, Bonnie Prince Charlie, laid rather desultory siege to the fortress in 1745, the elderly governor of the castle, General Preston, took to touring the defences in his bath chair, to keep the sentries on their toes. The only alarm came on the night of 25 September, but the scrambling noise heard out on the castle rock wasn't Jacobites, just goats grazing on the grassy tufts.

Tantallon Castle dominates the high cliffs east of North Berwick. Daniell conveys its drama wonderfully (*see above*); so too does his contemporary, Walter Scott, in his epic poem *Marmion*:

'…Tantallon vast,
Broad, massive, high and stretching far,
And held impregnable in war;
On a projecting rock it rose,
And round three sides the ocean flows,
The fourth did battled walls enclose …'

Sir William, first earl of Douglas, built Tantallon, probably to mark his elevation to the top flight of the Scottish nobility in 1358. The Douglases had been modest Lanarkshire landowners in the 12th century. But that all changed with William's uncle, Sir James of Douglas, nicknamed 'the Good'. So close was his friendship with Robert the Bruce that rich rewards came the family's way after Bruce became king. They included the barony of North Berwick. Tantallon was Earl William's way of announcing he had arrived. By creating a great curtain-walled castle, he was consciously looking back to the golden age of castle building in the preceding century.

TANTALLON CASTLE

East Lothian
Power house

In this, he was out of step with most of his peers, such as Sir William Keith, the grand marischal, at Dunnottar (*page 126*), who preferred a less ambitious, less costly residence centred on a rectangular tower house. Tantallon (*see above*) was the last great curtain-walled castle built from new in Scotland.

Above his front door, Earl William placed a stone plaque. Although badly worn, the heart carved thereon can still be made out. In its prime, that heart would have been painted blood red. Earl William's adoption of a heart as the family's chief armorial device displays his indebtedness to his Uncle James, who had been entrusted by Bruce to carry his heart to the Holy Land. That heart remains at the heart of the Douglas coat of arms to this day (*see right*).

The most conspicuous feature of Tantallon is the awesome red sandstone curtain wall drawn across the neck of the grassy headland. It now has a somewhat careworn appearance, having been battered not only by cannon but also by the winds and storms that are as much a part of this exposed spot as the rugged cliffs themselves. Its brute mass has just a narrow slit here and there lighting the wall chambers and access stairs behind. Three lofty towers projecting from the curtain housed the main residential accommodation (*see right*). The central tower contained the gateway at ground level and four upper floors, parts of which were almost certainly occupied by the constable. The Douglas Tower to the north (*see left*), with its seven floors, was Earl William's private lodging.

Behind the curtain wall lay the inner close, or courtyard. This would be the stage on which the Douglases would strut and sparkle. But things went awry following Earl William's death in 1384. Thanks to the shenanigans of his widow Margaret, countess of Angus, the Douglas story became a medieval 'soap opera'. The details need not concern us here; suffice to record that within four years the mighty house of Douglas had split into two, the 'Black' and the 'Red'. Tantallon passed to the Red Douglas earls of Angus, and remained their power house for the rest of its days. Tantallon was a great baronial residence, providing all the accommodation required by a powerful magnate. Rarely did it see action in wartime: Tantallon endured just three sieges in its 300-year existence as an active fortification – by James IV in 1491, James V in 1528 and Cromwell in 1651. The first was a damp squib of an affair. The last ripped open the lofty towers at either end of the curtain, rendering the place uninhabitable. James V's siege also caused extensive damage, but the repairs carried out after it have left an enduring mark on the ancient fabric.

The post-1528 siege repairs graphically illustrate the impact gunpowder had on medieval fortification after it first appeared in Scotland in the later 14th century. The problem now was the trajectory; at short range, guns (*such as the one illustrated above*) fired horizontally, not in the high looping arcs of the old trebuchets and mangonels. The result was that the walls were at risk, not just the battlements and roofs. On taking control of Tantallon, James ordered his masons to '*reinforce samin wallis quhilk* [which] *was left waist of befoir as transses and throuw passagis, and maid all massie* [massive] *work to that effect that it sould be unwinabill in tymes comming to ony enemies that would come to persew it'*. The truth of that statement is evident today. Thanks to the green conglomerate stone his masons used, easily distinguishable from the original red sandstone, we can see that the chambers in the great curtain were filled in, as well as the lower storeys of the south tower.

Most noticeably, a new fore tower (*see right*) was added to the entrance gate. The refortified castle was deemed 'of such strengthe' by the English in the 1540s that their ambassador used it as his base during the War of the Rough Wooing (*see page 137 for more information*). But such was the technological advance in gunpowdered artillery that by the time Cromwell besieged it a century later, the ancient power house had become antiquated, and was again vulnerable. Despite its post-1528 upgrade, Tantallon's curtain proved susceptible not to a frontal assault, but to bombardment from the flanks. In 1651 'the capitane and those few men who were with them betooke themselves to the tower, and resolved to sell their lives at as good rate as they could; but the enemy seeing them stand gallantly to it, preferred them quarter, which they accepted'. Thereby was mighty Tantallon, power house of the Red Douglases, saved from utter destruction.

BASS ROCK CASTLE

East Lothian
Scotland's Alcatraz

Two kilometres (1.25 miles) off the East Lothian coast, opposite Tantallon (*page 158*), the Bass Rock rises up like a giant boulder from the sea. (*The view seen right is from Tantallon.*) The Bass was made for birds, not humans – the very name comes from the Latin for gannet, *sula bassana* – and Daniell shows plenty of them circling overhead in his view (*see above*). They are still there: some 23,000 of them nest on the island. Viewed from a distance, the entire rock can be transformed from dull brown to brilliant white when the sun's rays shine on its carpet of guano.

People have also lived on the Bass, intermittently and mostly reluctantly. Legend tells that the hermit St Baldred had his retreat there long ago. In the 16th century the owner, Lauder of the Bass, built a castle to be used in tandem with Tantallon to protect the narrow sea channel running between. The importance of that passage was demonstrated as recently as 1995, during the Tall Ships' Race, when a sudden change in the wind forced them into taking that route when leaving the Forth. By then the lighthouse keepers, who had been on the Bass since 1902, had come and gone too.

The hermit, the castle garrison and the lighthouse keepers weren't the Bass's only inhabitants. Over three centuries ago, during the so-called 'killing time' in the 1670s and 1680s, Bass Rock was pressed into service as a state prison, to house the most problematic Covenanters (religious dissenters).

And there was no-one more problematic than the Rev. Alexander Peden, held there in the 1680s. Peden was expelled from his Wigtownshire parish in 1663 for refusing to renounce the Presbyterian Covenant. For the next ten years, he travelled around the south west ranting against Charles II's restoration. He became a sort of prophet among the 'hedge priests' (those who led open-air services or conventicles), and to evade capture he disguised his face with a mask (*see right*) that made him look as though he was horribly diseased. But the authorities finally caught up with him conducting a conventicle in Ayrshire in 1673, and brought him to the Bass, Scotland's Alcatraz. Peden became its main 'Bird Man'. For almost five years, Peden was forced to endure the privations of life on the Bass. He was allowed out of his cell for only a brief spell each day, to 'breathe the open air, and envy the birds their freedom', as he put it. During one spell, he reproached the prison governor for his addiction to gambling, prophesying: 'Sir, since you will not amend, the lord will strike you with a wound that will smite you to your very heart.' The story goes that, shortly after, the governor's young daughter was lifted bodily up by the wind and blown off the rock. The hermit, the garrison, the prisoners and lighthousemen have all come and gone. But still the birds remain, squawking at the day-trippers who dare to invade their space. Baldred's chapel, Lauder's castle and Peden's prison cell all now lie covered in that carpet of guano. *(The image on the left shows day-trippers from the turn of the twentieth century, pictured with the barren form of Bass Rock Castle looming in the background).*

BERWICK CASTLE

Northumberland
A bone between two dogs

The burgh of Berwick-upon-Tweed is English now, and has been officially these past five hundred years. On 24 August 1482, the Scots living there packed their bags for good. For well over four centuries before that, the neat town perched at the point where the River Tweed meets the North Sea had been Scottish – ever since that famous victory over the English at Carham, 24km (16 miles) upriver, in 1018. (*John Thomson's plan, right, was published in 1821*). It had all begun so brightly, for the town rapidly grew to be Scotland's largest and wealthiest; not strictly speaking a capital city, but probably the best known. But from that horrific day at Easter-tide 1296, when Edward I of England crossed the Tweed and butchered two-thirds of the population, the writing was on the wall. Abbot Walter of Inchcolm, in his *Scotichronicon*, wrote:

'For two days streams of blood flowed from the bodies of the slain so that mills could be turned round by the flow.'

The marvel is that the inhabitants endured another two hundred years of living in a war-zone before calling it a day. Between 1296 and 1482, Berwick-upon-Tweed passed back and forth between the warring countries much like a bone between two dogs, changing hands a total of at least 13 times during its history.

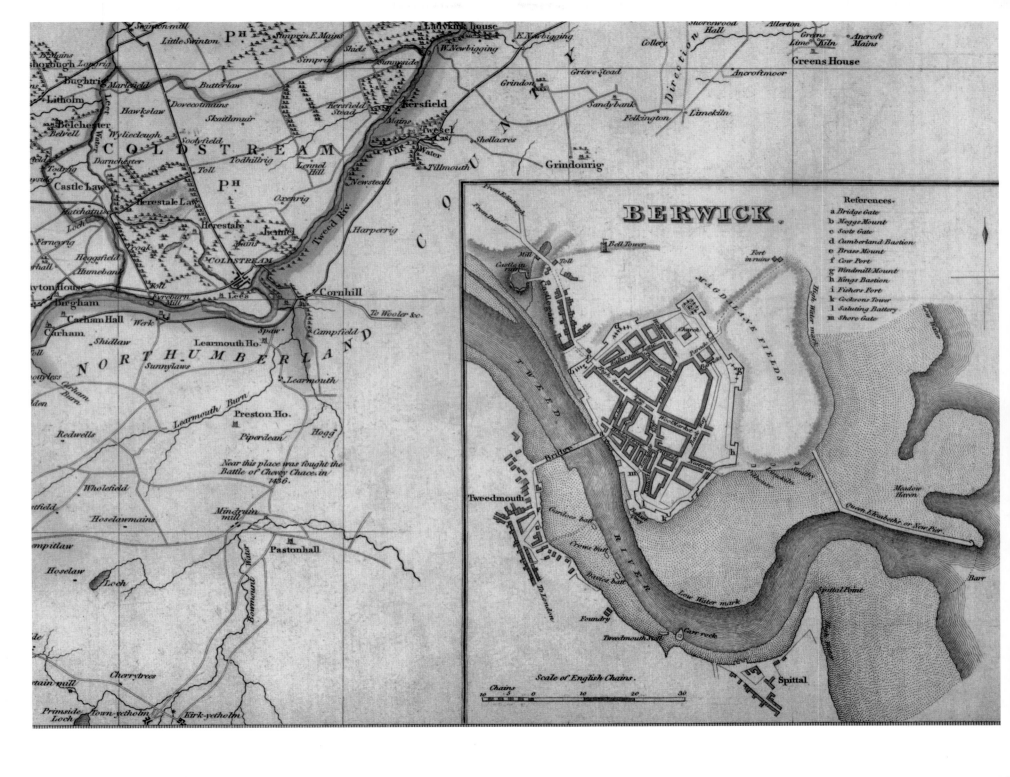

BERWICK.

References.
a Bridge Gate
b Meggs Mount
c Scots Gate
d Cumberland Bastion
e Brass Mount
f Cow Port
g Windmill Mount
h Kings Bastion
i Fishers Fort
k Cocksons Tower
l Saluting Battery
m Shore Gate

Scale of English Chains.

Chains
10   5   0   10   20   30

COLDSTREAM

NORTHUMBERLAND

COUNTY

Direction

Cornhill

Coldstream

Tweedmouth

Spittal

Ladykirk House

Greens House

Queen Elizabeths or New Pier

Meadow Haven

Spittal Point

Low Water mark

Carr rock

Tweedmouth Salt.

Foundry

Battice batt.

Crows batt.

Carlines batt.

To London

Tweed River

MAGDALENE FIELDS

High Water mark

Fort in ruins

Bell Tower

Castle in ruins

Mill
Toll

Church

Battery

WoolMarket

Bridge

Bridge St.

From Edinburgh

From Dunse

Near this place was fought the
Battle of Chevy Chace in
1436.

To Wooler &c.

The chief reason the inhabitants stayed was Berwick's strategic position right on the English Border. No bridges spanned the broad river way back then. Not until Edward IV of England took control in 1482 was the crossing bridged, by a wooden structure; the stone-arched 'herd of elephants' depicted by Daniell dates from after the Union of the Crowns in 1603. The castle was key to controlling that crossing.

Precious little remains of Berwick Castle physically (*the engraving above was published by Francis Grose in 1789 before the railway removed most of it in the 1840s*), but that it was one of the most important in Scotland is made abundantly clear in the written records. It was one of only three castles wrested from the Scots by Henry II of England in 1174 as ransom for William I 'the Lion' – the others were Roxburgh and Edinburgh (*page 150*); Richard I 'the Lionheart' only returned it 15 years later to help pay for his crusade

against Salah-ed-Din. In June 1291, a convocation of Scotland's great and good gathered in its great hall to debate the succession to the throne following the tragic deaths of Alexander II and his heir, Margaret the 'Maid of Norway'. The 'Great Cause', as the contest became known, dragged on for over a year and took many a twist and turn before the 12 contestants were whittled down to two: Robert Bruce (Robert I's grandfather) and John Balliol. On 17 November 1292 the judge, Edward I of England, found in favour of Balliol. But following Edward's return four years later, this royal seat of judgement fast declined into a border-control post. The town was corsetted in strong defences, beginning with Edward's own 'high dyke of turf' tipped with 'great long stakes'. The castle was recast in solid stone. Both countries contributed, as the 'bone' passed back and forth. A great gatehouse tower begun by Edward in 1303 was completed by King Robert Bruce after he recaptured the castle in 1318; Bruce

named it the Douglas Tower, in honour of his loyal companion, 'the Good' Sir James of Douglas (*see Tantallon page 158*). The English, who retook the castle in 1333, renamed it the Percy Tower, after Henry Percy, earl of Northumberland – nothing is forever, it seems. The Douglas/Percy Tower is certainly no more. In fact, apart from the west wall, only the stump of the Constable's Tower (*see right*) survives; this fine polygonal tower, with its fishtail arrow slits and well-built masonry, simply reminds us just how much we miss this once great royal 'bone'. Sadly, most of it was swept away with the coming of the railway in the 1840s. But next time you're standing on Platform 1 waiting for the 10.42 to Edinburgh Waverley, pause to reflect on the momentous event that happened on that spot on 17 November 1292 when Edward of England, 'Hammer of the Scots', finally pronounced in favour of King John Balliol. The rest is history, as they say!

GENERAL

M Coventry *The Castles of Scotland* (1997)
S Cruden *The Scottish Castle* (1981)
R Fawcett *Scottish Architecture from the Accession of the Stewarts to the Reformation 1371–1560* (1994)
D Howard *Scottish Architecture from the Reformation to the Restoration 1560–1660* (1995)
M Lindsay *The Castles of Scotland* (1986)
D MacGibbon & T Ross *The Castellated and Domestic Architecture of Scotland*, five vols (1887–92)
C Tabraham *Scotland's Castles* (2005)

INDIVIDUAL CASTLES

Caerlaverock Castle (page 10)
D Grove *Caerlaverock Castle* (HS official guide)
J Gifford *The Buildings of Scotland: Dumfries and Galloway* (1996), 140–50

MacLellan's Castle (page 16)
D Grove *Maclellan's Castle* (HS official guide)
J Gifford *The Buildings of Scotland: Dumfries and Galloway* (1996), 374–6

Cardoness Castle (page 22)
D Grove *Cardoness Castle and Carsluith Castle* (HS official aguide)
J Gifford *The Buildings of Scotland: Dumfries and Galloway* (1996), 157–9
W McCulloch *A History of the Galloway McCullochs* (1964)

Dunskey Castle (page 28)
J Gifford *The Buildings of Scotland: Dumfries and Galloway* (1996), 293–4

Dumbarton Castle (page 34)
I MacIvor *Dumbarton Castle* (HS official guide)
I MacPhail *Dumbarton Castle* (1979)

Lochranza Castle (page 42)
R McLellan *The Ancient Monuments of Arran* (HS official guide)

Inveraray Castle (page 48)
RCAHMS *Inventory of Argyll, volume 7: Mid Argyll and Cowal* (1992), no. 184
F A Walker *The Buildings of Scotland: Argyll and Bute* (2000), 313–23

Castle Sween (page 54)
RCAHMS *Inventory of Argyll, volume 7: Mid Argyll and Cowal* (1992), no. 119
F A Walker *The Buildings of Scotland: Argyll and Bute* (2000), 184–7

Dunollie Castle (page 60)
RCAHMS *Inventory of Argyll, volume 2: Lorn* (1975), no. 286
F A Walker *The Buildings of Scotland: Argyll and Bute* (2000), 421–2

Dunstaffnage Castle (page 66)
D Grove *Dunstaffnage Castle and Chapel* (HS official guide)
RCAHMS *Inventory of Argyll, volume 2: Lorn* (1975), no. 287
F A Walker *The Buildings of Scotland: Argyll & Bute* (2000), 237–42

Aros Castle (page 72)
RCAHMS *Inventory of Argyll, volume 3: Mull, Tiree, Coll and Northern Argyll* (1980), no. 333
F A Walker *The Buildings of Scotland: Argyll and Bute* (2000), 313–23

Mingary Castle (page 78)
J Gifford *The Buildings of Scotland: Highlands and Islands* (1992), 257–60
RCAHMS *Inventory of Argyll, volume 3: Mull, Tiree, Coll and Northern Argyll* (1980), no. 345

Eilean Donan Castle (page 84)
J Gifford *The Buildings of Scotland: Highlands and Islands* (1992), 532–4
R Miket & D Roberts *The Mediaeval Castles of Skye & Lochalsh* (1990), 74–92

Caisteal Maol (page 88)
J Gifford *The Buildings of Scotland: Highlands and Islands* (1992), 542–3

FURTHER READING

R Miket & D Roberts *The Mediaeval Castles of Skye & Lochalsh* (1990), 32–8

Dunvegan Castle (page 92)
J Gifford *The Buildings of Scotland: Highlands and Islands* (1992), 527–32
R Miket & D Roberts *The Mediaeval Castles of Skye & Lochalsh* (1990), 65–73

Bishop's Palace, Kirkwall (page 96)
J Gifford *The Buildings of Scotland: Highlands and Islands* (1992), 327–9
W D Simpson *The Bishop's Palace and Earl's Palace* (HS official guide)

Earl's Palace, Kirkwall (page 102)
J Gifford *The Buildings of Scotland: Highlands and Islands* (1992), 329–32
W D Simpson *The Bishop's Palace and Earl's Palace* (HS official guide)
P D Anderson *Black Patie: The Life and Times of Patrick, Earl of Orkney, Lord of Shetland* (1992)

Castle Girnigoe (page 108)
J Gifford *The Buildings of Scotland: Highlands and Islands* (1992), 109–12

Castle of Old Wick (page 110)
C E Batey 'Viking and Late Norse Caithness: The Archaeological Evidence', *Proceedings of the Tenth Viking Congress* (1985), 131–48
J Gifford *The Buildings of Scotland: Highlands and Islands* (1992), 113

Dunrobin Castle (page 114)
E Beaton *Sutherland: An Illustrated Architectural Guide* (1995), 53–5
J Gifford *The Buildings of Scotland: Highlands and Islands* (1992), 570–77

Dornoch Castle (page 118)
R Fawcett *Scottish Cathedrals* (1997)
J Gifford *The Buildings of Scotland: Highlands and Islands* (1992), 568–9

Kinnairdhead Castle (page122)
J Leslie & R Paxton *Bright Lights: The Stevenson Engineers 1752–1971* (1999)

Dunnottar Castle (page 126)
W D Simpson *Dunnottar Castle* (1983)
C Burnett & C Tabraham *The Honours of Scotland* (1993)

Broughty Castle (page 134)
F Mudie et al *Broughty Castle and the Defence of the Tay* (1970)

St Andrews Castle (page 142)
R Fawcett *St Andrews Castle* (HS official guide)
J Gifford *The Buildings of Scotland: Fife* (1988), 369–72

Edinburgh Castle (page 150)
J Gifford et al *The Buildings of Scotland: Edinburgh* (1984), 85–102
I MacIvor *Edinburgh Castle* (1993)
RCAHMS *Inventory of Edinburgh* (1951), no. 1
C Tabraham *Edinburgh Castle* (HS official guide)

Tantallon Castle (page 158)
W Fraser *The Douglas Books*, four vols (1885)
C Tabraham & D Grove *Tantallon Castle* (HS official guide)

Bass Rock Castle (page 164)
C McWilliam *The Buildings of Scotland: Lothian* (1978), 94–5

Berwick Castle (page 168)
D Grove *Berwick Barracks and Fortifications* (English Heritage official guide)
C Strang *Borders and Berwick: An Illustrated Guide* (1994), 5–19

The author is grateful to the following people for their help:

Professor David Breeze, Chief Inspector of Ancient Monuments, Historic Scotland; Dr Allan Rutherford, Inspector of Ancient Monuments, Historic Scotland; Ms Bryony Coombs, Assistant Photographic Librarian, Historic Scotland; Ms Lynn Earley, Photographic Library, RCAHMS

PICTURE CREDITS

Crown Copyright reproduced courtesy of Historic Scotland: 14, 15, 17, 18, 19, 20, 21, 23, 24, 25, 26, 27, 35, 36, 39, 40, 41, 43, 44, 45 (both), 46, 47, 49, 52, 53, 55, 56, 59, 61, 63, 67, 68, 69, 70, 71, 79, 80, 81, 85, 90, 91, 93, 95, 97, 98, 100, 101, 103, 104, 105, 106, 107, 111, 112, 120, 121, 125, 127, 128 (all), 130, 131, 132, 133, 135, 136, 138, 139, 140, 143, 144, 145, 146, 147, 148, 149, 151, 155, 156, 157, 159 (both), 160, 161, 162, 163, 165, 170, 171.
Reproduced © Royal Commission on the Ancient and Historical Monuments of Scotland: 11, 29, 30, 33, 50, 62, 64, 65, 74, 75, 76, 77, 82, 83, 84, 94, 109, 115, 117, 119, 123, 124, 166.
Reproduced by permission of the Trustees National Library of Scotland: Images from William Daniell *A Voyage around Great Britain undertaken between the years 1813 and 1823 and commencing from the Land's End, Cornwall, with a series of views illustrative of the character and prominent features of the coast drawn and engraved by William Daniell*, first edition London (1814–25), reprinted London (1978): 10, 16, 22, 28, 32, 34, 42, 48, 54, 60, 66, 72, 78, 84, 88, 92, 96, 102, 108, 110, 114, 116, 118, 122, 126, 134, 142, 150, 158, 164, 168. *Anandale*, Herman Moll (1745) 12. *Profile of the Front of the Castle of Island Dounan*, Lewis Petit (1708) 86. *Berwick-Shire*, John Thomson (1821) 169.
© Trustees of the National Museum of Scotland: 37, 167.
Colin Baxter: 13, 89.
© The Duke of Roxburgh: Image of King David I & Malcolm IV from Charter to Kelso Abbey (1159) 152.
Dundee City Museums Collection: 141.
By permission of Sir Robert M Clerk of Penicuik Bt: *Old Inveraray Castle and Old Inveraray Burgh view from the SE*, Clerk of Eldin (c. 1770) 51

REFERENCES

Page 12: see C Scott-Giles *The Siege of Caerlaverock*, London (1960)
Page 22: quoted in Sir Andrew Agnew of Lochnaw *Hereditary Sheriffs of Galloway*, ii, page 19, Edinburgh (1893)
Page 80: P Gordon *A Short Abridgement of Britane's Distemper*, Spalding Club (1844), 65
Page 95: J Boswell *Journal of a Tour to the Hebrides with Samuel Johnson 1773*, reprinted by Canongate Classics, Edinburgh (1998)
Page 99: quoted in A O Anderson *Early Sources of Scottish History*, Edinburgh (1922)
Page 102: quoted in P D Anderson *Black Patie: The Life and Times of Patrick, Earl of Orkney, Lord of Shetland* (1992)
Page 137: quoted in F Mudie et al *Broughty Castle and the Defence of the Tay* (1970)
Page 141: quoted in F Mudie et al *Broughty Castle and the Defence of the Tay* (1970)
Page 149: see J Brewer et al, *Letters and Papers, Foreign and Domestic, Henry VIII*, vol. xxi, part ii, no. 380, London (1864)
Page 154: see P Hume Brown *Early Travellers in Scotland*, Edinburgh (1978)
Page 158: see Sir Walter Scott *The Works of Sir Walter Scott*, Wordsworth poetry library (1995)
Page 162: R Lindesay of Pitscottie *The Historie and Cronicles of Scotland*, i, 330–33 (Scottish Text Society, 1899)
Page 162: Sir James Balfour's *Annales*; see *The Historical Works of Sir James Balfour*, Edinburgh (1825)
Page 167: A Peden *The Life and Prophecies of the Reverend Mr Alexander Peden*, Falkirk (1686?)
Page 168: quoted in D E R Watt (ed) *A History Book for Scots: selections from Scotichronicon*, Edinburgh (1998)

ACKNOWLEDGEMENTS

INDEX